BEYOND TH
GATE

BEYOND THE SCHOOL GATE

*A parents' guide to primary schools and the
National Curriculum*

Wendy and David Clemson

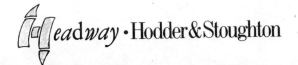
eadway · Hodder & Stoughton

This book is for our parents,
Marjorie and Bertie and Eva and Bill.

British Library Cataloguing in Publication Data
Clemson, Wendy
  Beyond the school gate: a parents' guide to primary
  schools and the National Curriculum. – (Headway).
  1. Great Britain. Primary schools. Curriculum
  I. Title II. Clemson, David
  372.190941

  ISBN 0 340 53672 1

First published 1990

© 1990 Wendy and David Clemson

Phototypeset by Input Typesetting Ltd, London.
Printed in Great Britain for the educational publishing division of
Hodder and Stoughton Ltd, Mill Road, Dunton Green, Sevenoaks,
Kent by Clays Ltd, St Ives plc.

CONTENTS

PREFACE

T here is nothing more important than the education of young children, and we believe that all adults should be actively engaged in promoting educational opportunities for children, both in and out of school. Our concern in this book is to help parents understand what is happening in primary schools, in the hope that teachers and parents can then offer children enjoyable and profitable schooldays under the National Curriculum.

We approach the National Curriculum with optimism. That does not mean we fully support all that must be done in schools. However, the National Curriculum is now law, and children, parents and teachers must accommodate it, whilst seeing it as providing opportunities for creative interpretation.

At times it is difficult to avoid being over-earnest about schools and schooling. We have too much investment in our daughters and sons for us to be light-hearted. But we must try to ensure that learning is 'fun' whilst remembering that anything worthwhile involves hard work. Only if we remember that the purpose of schooling is to open opportunities and not close options, will we make the National Curriculum work. We wish you well in your support for your children for, though their future is now in our hands, it is the future of the world that will be in theirs.

INTRODUCTION

The introduction of a National Curriculum for children aged five to sixteen years in State schools is the most significant change in education since 1944. It was then that an Education Act was passed which set up the system of primary, secondary and further education that we have today. However, we have to go back 150 years to find the most recent clear prescription for the content of our school curriculum.

The main reasons why we have a National Curriculum now are that politicians feel it will remedy what they see as people's concerns about:

- standards
- sloppy and lackadaisical attitudes to learning in school; and
- the difficulties in continuing learning at the appropriate point when children transfer from one school to another.

STANDARDS

We all talk about and many of us hold strong views on standards in education. Commonly the standards we think of are in terms of English and mathematics. The old 'three Rs', reading, writing and arithmetic, are still the major concern of most parents. Surveys seem to suggest that parents are concerned about standards nationally, but that most parents seem to be satisfied with their child's progress in the local primary school. In other words, parents have a poor opinion of standards in schools nationally, but have a high opinion of the standards in the school they know.

Whether or not standards have risen or fallen is a matter for discussion; it depends what your standards are and how you measure them. It is enough here to say that our children have far more knowledge available to them than any of us had when we were schoolchildren. This information explosion needs to be recognised in any consideration of standards. We doubt that education for one generation was ever 'right' for the next. Now it is definitely not the case that what was good enough for us is good enough for our children. What was taught in A level syllabuses fifteen years ago is now taught to children well before their GCSE.

The fact that there is more knowledge has two repercussions. The first is that the balance of the amount of knowledge and depth of learning needs to be constantly monitored. The second is that many decisions have to be made about what to leave out of school learning. To do this the writers of the National Curriculum have had to select those things which they see as being fundamental to a subject and to place these basic learning steps in an order which will allow children to become progressively more knowledgeable. For example, in mathematics, pupils should learn to add and subtract to 10 before they add and subtract to 20 and use 0. (These are in Attainment Target 3, Levels 2 and 3). Additionally, pupils should know words needed for measuring, like 'longer' and 'shorter' etc. before they tackle common units of measurement like metres and litres. (These are in Attainment Target 8, Levels 1 and 2).

THE PACE OF SCHOOL LEARNING

The other motivating force behind the National Curriculum is the desire to step up the pace of activity in schools. There is a feeling that more can be achieved. This feeling relates both to the time children spend on their work and to the learning structures that a school offers to the children. There is evidence that the more time children spend on their work the more they achieve and succeed in that work. Whilst the National Curriculum statements do not prescribe actual hours of the week to be spent on each subject or topic, there is guidance about this. It is likely that we will see schools adopting very similar patterns of time allocation. This may also mean that such things as the time and length of assemblies, playtimes, and lunch hours will perhaps be reduced and become the same in many schools.

The question of discipline is often confused by ideas to do with punishment. It is important to distinguish between discipline in the sense of dealing with children who play up in class and the discipline of learning. Whilst a disruptive child is preventing his own learning and that of his classmates, it would be a mistake to assume that the quiet child is a disciplined learner. It is necessary for children to learn about learning and how to study. The National Curriculum writers make it clear that teachers must make sure children are taught how to learn. The increase in pace in school will make the teaching and learning of study skills an imperative. It will produce younger independent learners. This means that young children will start to organise their own learning and find out their best ways of working.

A COMMON PLAN THROUGH THE YEARS OF SCHOOLING

When we look at the opportunities for learning given to children under the National Curriculum, each subject is set out as a list of knowledge items. The list starts with the first things they should learn and these are labelled Level 1. The items on the list seem to become more complex through the Levels because they build on the previous Levels, until Level 10 is reached.

At first, the Levels were conceived to match the ten years of each child's compulsory schooling. However, as the details of each subject were worked out, the match Level for year was not maintained. Children who perform above or below average, may not work on a Level per year basis. The Levels worked at by secondary school children will markedly vary from the year per Level idea. We all do better in some subjects, and not so well in others. It is the teachers' job to see that our children get the opportunity to work at their optimum, *at whatever Level that may be*. And we must expect the Level to vary, perhaps, from subject to subject, and even from one part of a subject to another.

What is important is that now we have a national system, the transition from one class or teacher to another, and from one school to another should be more straightforward. After all, all teachers in all State schools in England and Wales are working on the same minimum curriculum.

— I —

WHAT IS THE NATIONAL CURRICULUM?

A NEW LAW

T he National Curriculum is a schooling revolution for everyone between the ages of five and sixteen and probably beyond. It is part of a new law, passed in 1988, called the Education Reform Act. It requires a number of important and far reaching changes to be made throughout the education system. These will mean real and lasting effects upon schools and, of course, the opportunities and experiences offered to our children. The first stages of the National Curriculum were introduced into schools in the Autumn Term 1989.

Whilst the Education Reform Act was introduced by the Conservative Government, with Kenneth Baker as the Secretary of State for Education and Science at the time, the roots of the National Curriculum stretch back over the last twenty years. During that time, our system of education and the outcomes of that system have been increasingly placed under the microscope. The National Curriculum can be seen as a logical outcome of that scrutiny by all political parties. This has produced a growing appreciation and political consensus that a National Curriculum should be seen as a framework for our children's education and not as a narrow prescription. Members of the National Curriculum Council, the body created by the Government to implement the Act, are already saying that they will welcome discussion about the revision of content as the experience of teaching and learning under the National Curriculum grows.

From our viewpoint as parents, although the Education Reform Act contains sweeping changes, the three most important aspects are:

– a National Curriculum for all;
– regular assessment and testing; and
– regular reporting to parents.

A CHANGE IN WHAT MUST BE TAUGHT

Before the new law was passed, the only thing teachers were legally required to teach was religious education. Of course, most teachers covered a wide range of skills and ideas in many subjects, but there were differences between what each teacher and school offered five- to sixteen-year-olds. A National Curriculum for all means that there will now be public documents that set out what teachers must teach, and this has been extended from just RE, to comprise a list of subjects called 'Foundation subjects'. These, along with RE, are the very least to be offered to all children. What it means is that parents, teachers and everyone else can read what is the minimum that the children should have the chance to learn in any State school in England and Wales.

The official documents setting out the National Curriculum are called Statutory Orders. All schools will have at least one complete set of all of these documents. They contain:

What teachers are expected to teach: **Programmes of Study**
What children should have the chance to learn: **Attainment Targets (ATs)**

Some of the official documents about what should happen in schools have already been published. Our advice is not to

buy them. They are long, indigestible, and under constant review. If you would like to consult them, you can ask to see a copy in school, or your local reference library can obtain them for you.

SUBJECTS

We are all used to describing our school experiences in terms of subjects and this is how the National Curriculum is described. The subjects are called **Foundation** subjects, three of which are Core. The Core subjects are:

English,
mathematics, and
science.

The other Foundation subjects are:

technology (including design),
history,
geography,
music,
art, and
PE,

(and for secondary school children, a modern foreign language).

Whilst the Curriculum is described in terms of subjects, the National Curriculum Council have made clear to schools that these subjects do not make up the whole curriculum offered to our children. Primary schools must also take account of gender and multicultural issues, special educational needs, information technology and personal and social education. Personal and social education includes health education, environmental education and economic and industrial understanding.

STAGES AND AGES

The years of schooling have been divided into four stages:

Key Stage 1 includes five- to seven-year-olds
Key Stage 2 includes seven- to eleven-year-olds
Key Stages 3 and 4 apply to secondary school children.

In many schools the children are in year group classes. That is where birthdates from 1 September to 31 August in the following year are the cut-off points for each class. Here the classes may come to be known as R, Y1, Y2, Y3, Y4, Y5, Y6.

If we set the classes out year by year, they look like this:

Class	Year	Ages	Key Stage
Reception	R	4–5	1 (only the 5–year-olds)
Middle Infant	Y1	5–6	1
Top Infant	Y2	6–7	1
Lower Junior	Y3	7–8	2
	Y4	8–9	2
Upper Junior	Y5	9–10	2
	Y6	10–11	2

It is likely that our children will continue to have a class-teacher for a year at a time due to a concern for security and a settled environment. However, it is probable that some of the time there will be team teaching and the sharing of experiences with children and teachers from other classes. This does happen in some schools already, but this kind of work may increase.

TARGETS

Each Foundation subject is divided into a number of **Attainment Targets**. For example, in English there are five Attainment Targets: Speaking and Listening, Reading, Writing, Spelling and Handwriting. Each Attainment Target is a list of things that children should have the chance to learn, arranged cumulatively in Levels. In most Attainment Targets there are ten Levels. The Levels are intended to cover all the years of every child's compulsory schooling. For most of our children in primary schools, we will be concerned with Levels up to and possibly including Level 5. If our children master work at this Level, then their teachers should ensure that they have access to Level 6 and so on. So, if we look at English AT 1, Speaking and Listening:

Level 1 says, for example:
   '. . . respond appropriately to simple instructions given by a teacher.'

Level 2 includes:
   '. . . respond appropriately to a range of more complex instructions given by a teacher, and give simple instructions.'

and Level 3:
   '. . . give, receive and follow accurately, precise instructions when pursuing a task individually or as a member of a group.'

(*English in the National Curriculum* (1989). DES and the Welsh Office, pp. 3 & 4.)

The numbers of Attainment Targets varies from subject to subject. Mathematics, for example, has fourteen.

LEVELS

All the discussion of Levels can be rather confusing. The Levels are steps in learning, but there are no rules about the rate at which children should move from one Level to the next. The people who have written the documents relating to the Core subjects have come up with what they feel is the likely range of Levels at each Key Stage in each Core subject. Their suggestions are these:

in English:
    Key Stage 1   Levels 1–3
    Key Stage 2   Levels 2–5

in mathematics:
    Key Stage 1   Levels 1–3
    Key Stage 2   Levels 2–6

in science:
    Key Stage 1   Levels 1–3
    Key Stage 2   Levels 2–5

As parents, we must remember that the Attainment Targets are actually lists of items that children should have the chance to learn. In other words they have more to do with the subject than the learner. The learning child is not the most important consideration. The cut-off points for the Levels are often conceptual ones in the subject and not related to ages and stages for real children. This may sound a harsh criticism of the way the whole idea of children's learning has been approached, but it does help us to maintain a sense of

perspective about our own children's progress. Human beings are too complex to be placed in 'boxes', 'compartments' or at 'levels' with any ease. The Levels of the National Curriculum are a framework within and around which children and teachers have to work.

Our concerns should be whether our children are 'learning at their best', at whatever Level or Levels that may be. And there should be full and equal opportunities to work, right across the curriculum, for all children.

WHO IS ACCOUNTABLE?

The Department of Education and Science, which is drawing on the recommendations of working groups and expert organisations, is responsible for the documents setting out the content of the National Curriculum. The local education authorities and their inspectors and advisers are responsible for giving teachers support and training (in-service training or INSET) to make the National Curriculum work.

Headteachers have to steer their schools through a programme of planning and of deciding how to deliver the whole curriculum in their school. They have to see that a school National Curriculum development plan is prepared. Classteachers must teach at least what is set out in the National Curriculum, and assess children's progress adequately.

Governors have a range of duties in collaboration with the headteacher. Whilst there has always been a form of governing body for our schools, the Act brings what must be their concerns into much sharper focus. These responsibilities are considerably increased and with them the power of the governors. It is partly for this reason that governors are now clearly accountable to us, the parents, and have to provide regular reports. This is why there is a requirement for elected parent governors to be on all governing bodies.

WHAT GOVERNORS MUST DO

The new law makes the job of a school governor an arduous and important one. Governors have to:

- be familiar with all aspects of the National Curriculum;

- understand the new assessment arrangements;

- keep up to date with National Curriculum developments;

- take action to implement the requirements of the National Curriculum and its assessment arrangements;

- ensure the provision of religious education and acts of collective worship;

- increasingly assume responsibility for the budgetary arrangements and expenditure of the school; and

- provide information to parents and the local education authority.

This is a formidable list and one which is not to be taken on lightly. The assumption of responsibility, for example, for the school's annual budget, will mean that governors are going to have to decide how to spend the school's money, and where, if necessary, to make savings. It is the governors who will decide, for example, whether to reduce the stationery bill or the number of teachers. Knowing that they make decisions as important as this will make us all more circumspect when voting for parent governors.

ASSESSMENT UNDER THE NATIONAL CURRICULUM

Children are assessed to discover their progress and problems. With the advent of the National Curriculum the assessments will be more systematic than they have sometimes been in the past, and will be set to an external standard. Teachers and schools will need to look continuously at how children are getting on in relation to the National Curriculum. They may also look at other learning that they see as important, such as study skills, social maturity and so on.

At the age of seven, and again at eleven, children in schools throughout England and Wales will be given special tests to assess their progress. Teachers have always seen assessment as part of their job, and now teachers' own assessments will be added to the results of national tests to give a picture of how each child is progressing. The assessment of your child's progress will therefore be arrived at through a combination of national tests and teacher assesssments.

REPORTING UNDER THE NATIONAL CURRICULUM

Results of national tests, taken at age seven and eleven, will go to parents. The first reported tests for seven-year-olds

are due in 1992, and for eleven-year-olds in 1995. The first group whose test results will be reported to parents at age eleven are those born between 1 September 1983 and 31 August 1984. If your children were born after 31 August 1984, they should take the national tests at seven and eleven and the results will come to you.

However, this does not mean that you will only get 'reports' at those times. Individual education authorities and schools have different policies about reporting progress. Some may already recommend and compile 'reports' every year.

You now have a legal right to information about your children's progress. This information includes test results and, for comparison, a profile of results for the class as a whole. Your children's individual results are confidential between you, your children and the teachers. Aggregate test results for eleven-year-olds must be published, but schools are not obliged to publish these figures for seven-year-olds.

You can find out how your children are getting on at school at any time, and there is some advice about how to go about it in Chapter 3. In fact, if you are at all concerned it is better to ask than to worry. Children often seem to tap what their parents feel about school, even without anything being said.

NEW 'MUSTS' FOR SCHOOLS

Schools must:

- have a National Curriculum plan;

- implement the National Curriculum for Key Stage 1 (starting with the five-year-olds) in September 1989;

- implement the National Curriculum for Key Stage 2 (starting with the seven-year-olds) in September 1990;

- test children at the end of Key Stage 1, starting in 1991;

- test children at the end of Key Stage 2, starting in 1994;

- report to parents on children's progress at seven and eleven, starting with seven-year-olds in 1992 and eleven-year-olds in 1995; and

- compile a public report on how all the eleven-year-olds in the school are progressing, in other words an overall achievements report which may include information about the area where the school is situated.

SUMMARY

The introduction of a National Curriculum and its assessment arrangements, together with the transfer of budgets to governing bodies, are the most significant changes in our education system for the last fifty years. They will have much more impact and long-term effects than such things as the development of comprehensive schools, or the introduction of GCSE. The new arrangements for schooling are the springboard for the future and they are the structures on which we will journey into the twenty-first century.

It is vital, therefore, that all of us take an active interest in our children's educational opportunities and how they are framed. By this we mean being involved in the education of all children. The first step in active involvement is to understand what the National Curriculum is all about. The rest of this book is devoted to providing the information to help our participation in children's education, to serve their best interests as starter learners for life.

— 2 —

HOW THE NATIONAL CURRICULUM MAY CHANGE LESSONS

THE HEART OF THE CURRICULUM: THE THREE RS AND MORE

T hroughout history, there has been an understanding in schools of the most important things that should be taught. There has been little shift over the centuries concerning the focus of school lesson time. In England and Wales, for at least the last 100 years, the 'three Rs' of reading, writing and arithmetic have been seen as the central subjects for teaching, along with religious education. It is these that have taken up a sizeable proportion of lesson time. The intention has been that children should achieve basic literacy, numeracy and some religious and moral instruction. As parents of the 1990s, we still have little quarrel with that idea of a basic education. In the National Curriculum, religious education still appears but is no longer at the heart of the curriculum. This is a formal acknowledgment of increased responsibility of the State for schooling, over and above that of the churches. The religious content of the curriculum may be an issue for some of us, but literacy and numeracy are seen as vital by everyone.

In the National Curriculum, literacy and numeracy are given 'core' status but are broader in content than the subjects studied fifty years ago. In English, speaking and listening are added to the traditional skills of reading and writing. Mathematics is seen as having two strands. The first is about number, algebra and measures. The second concerns shape, space and data handling. The new addition to the core of the curriculum is science, which includes a study of methods used in scientific enquiry and knowledge to be learned.

THE CORE SUBJECTS: ENGLISH

First and foremost

Language is what we think in! It is the thread that permeates all the other subjects. Lack of progress in English holds back work in other subjects. And we do not have a single 'way with language' that fits all subjects, ways of writing or audiences. We do not speak English in the way we write it. We do not write to auntie in the way we write up a science experiment. Non-fiction books are often different in style from novels. At school we are expecting children to work out all these differences, and more, and operate them themselves.

Looking at the National Curriculum documents that tell teachers what should be taught and what the children should have the opportunity to learn, the skills and knowledge of English have been set out in five sections. These sections are the Attainment Targets for English and are as follows:

Speaking and listening	(AT 1)
Reading	(AT 2)
Writing	(AT 3)
Spelling	(AT 4)
Handwriting	(AT 5)

But these Attainment Targets do not indicate what our children will experience in their classrooms. Teachers are going to have to translate these into real learning opportunities. It is the different ways in which this translation will take place that will lead to the differences between schools. So what sorts of things will we find our children doing?

What this means for English lessons

Both parents and teachers tend to measure progress in English through reading and writing. The National Curriculum gives due emphasis to these, but will make all of us think much more about the value of speaking and listening. The quality of our children's English work will depend upon there being a balanced set of activities which allow oral work alongside written work; both of these being supported and extended through reading. English lessons, then, will involve talk, children moving around, group work, drafting of written work, the reading of non-fiction as well as fiction books, and the development of presentation skills. The sorts of skills and knowledge expected from our children, in English, can best be illustrated by looking at a range of children and their work in each of the Attainment Targets.

Speaking and listening Marina is just six and in a middle infant class. She is working on Level 1, where it is expected that she should be able to:

- speak and listen while at work or play in a group;

- listen to and respond to stories and poems; and

- carry out the teacher's instructions (for example, get a book and sit and look at it).

Marina is a typical six-year-old in that she is operating at Level 1. She will have spent all her life listening and learning to communicate, and her vocabulary will have been dependent upon, for example, the amount of talking she has done with the adults in her life. In school she is now learning not only reading and writing but also the appropriateness of particular talk, the importance of listening and of asking questions, and how to share ideas through discussion. All of these are extremely important skills for everyday communication in all the things that we do.

Reading Dan is nearly eight and in a first year junior class working towards Level 3. He will soon be able to:

- read aloud a poem or story he knows with fluency and expression;

- read silently;

- listen to a story and retell the details of it;

- show reading skills like anticipating story outcomes and understanding meanings which are not literal;

- show in his writing and discussion about stories that he knows about their structure (beginnings and endings and so on); and

- choose and use reference books, having decided what he wants to find out.

Dan is 'in-between' Levels. He has mastered Levels 1 and 2 and is now being extended in his reading. Dan should reach Level 4, and perhaps Level 5, in his primary schooling. The important message underpinning the development of reading is that there are a variety of skills which need to be acquired for mastery. Only one of these is the ability to speak the words on the page. Dan will also need to be able to choose books for different purposes, make links between ideas in different books, and know how to tackle difficult vocabulary and ideas.

Writing Amy is a top infant, soon to be seven, and has achieved Level 2. She can now do all of these things:

- write on her own, using sentences, capital letters and full stops;

- write a story or, for example, write up a mathematics activity with events in the right order;

- show she knows a little about stories having a structure by giving a written story a start, characters and events; and

- write things other than stories, like shopping lists and captions.

Through her writing, and in other activities, Amy, who has also achieved Level 2 in spelling and handwriting can show that she can do these things:

Spelling
- spell recognisably, if not correctly, lots of common words;

- spell correctly short words she uses regularly;

- use spelling patterns to work out spellings; and

- say the names and order of letters in the alphabet.

Handwriting
- use capital and small letters; and

- write letters recognisably and the correct way around.

In order that the children are able to learn all the things in the lists above (and more), their teachers have to give them a range of tasks and activities to do. As each child works on from one Level to the next, the activities will seen more complex, for they draw on all the children's past knowledge and work.

It is small wonder that English takes up a lot of school time. As our examples about individual children show, the reading and writing of our schooldays have been worked out in fine detail. Compared with the experience of some of us, much more ground is now covered in English. Speaking and listening is an important addition, so some English work will include talk (not idle chatter), structured discussion, and speaking to an audience. Even in classes and schools where the teacher is the one who has talked the most, time will now have to be found for children to talk too.

THE CORE SUBJECTS: MATHEMATICS

Fun with numbers, patterns, problems and more

For many of us the word 'mathematics' makes us think 'sums'. In fact doing sums is only a part of mathematics. The whole subject is '. . . a means for organising, communicating and manipulating information. . .' using '. . . diagrams and symbols with associated conventions and theorems. The special power of mathematics lies in its capacity to suggest possible answers to practical problems.' (*Mathematics for ages 5 to 16* (1988) Proposals of the Secretary of State for Education and Science and the Secretary of State for Wales, p. 3.) This definition of mathematics gives us some idea of the kinds of things our children do in school when maths is on the timetable.

Mathematics is the subject many of us hated at school. There are lots of reasons for our feelings, and some of these may include the way mathematics was taught. We learned to do things with numbers without understanding what we were doing. All that mattered was the tick for the answer. Also, some bits of mathematics seemed separate from the things we do in everyday life, and not at all useful. All the skills for doing the shopping, measuring up for a new carpet and interpreting the railway timetable are there in the National Curriculum, and they are not 'hidden' as they were in our mathematics books. The tie-in with everyday life is still not complete, however, and that is as it should be. Working with numbers and patterns can be for fun, and mathematicians, whether beginners or working at an advanced level, can develop communication, reasoning and problem-solving skills as well as creativity through their mathematics.

With these ideas in mind it is easier to understand why writers of the National Curriculum for mathematics included fourteen sections or Attainment Targets. Infants work on Attainment Targets 1–6 and 8–14. Juniors work on all fourteen Attainment Targets. The fourteen Attainment Targets can be grouped into five main areas of mathematics.

Number	(ATs 2, 3, 4 and 5)
Algebra	(ATs 5, 6 and 7)
Measures	(AT 8)
Shape and space	(ATs 10 and 11)
Handling data	(ATs 12, 13 and 14)

All of these areas are to be supported by the 'methods of mathematics' Attainment Targets, Using and Applying Mathematics (ATs 1 and 9). This means that our children are now expected to know not only how to work with numbers and symbols and how to measure things, but also to work on such things as symmetry and co-ordinates and use a computer for pattern making and geometrical constructions. They then need to be able to use all this knowledge in solving problems.

To illustrate the sorts of things our youngsters are doing it is useful to look at some typical situations.

What this means for mathematics lessons

Children may work alone, in pairs, or sometimes in a group on their mathematics. They may move about the school as they fetch resources or do a practical activity. They may do some of their work with children from another class or with another teacher. The teacher may approach the work in a straightforward linear fashion, that is by tackling work leading to a Level in Attainment Target 2 before working on that same Level for Attainment Target 3. She may use the Attainment Target material more flexibly than that by finding an appropriate route through the Targets for her class, or bunching related Targets together and treating them as a module for learning. However she does it, her intention must be to give all the children the best possible chances to learn.

Here is the work of some typical children who are operating at various Levels within the five main mathematical areas.

Number Frances is six. She is approaching Level 2 in her Number work where she is expected to:

- know her numbers up to 100;

- do simple addition and subtraction up to 10;

- understand halves and quarters;

- make sensible estimations of numbers of things up to 20; and

- do simple addition and subtraction with money.

All of this is not a recipe for pages of 'add' and 'take away' sums. Frances should be handling objects and play money. She should be playing games which require simple computation and counting on and back. She will need to be dividing real things into halves and quarters.

Algebra Alik is ten. He is at Level 4 which is the Level that many primary children are likely to be at at his age. In Algebra he is expected to be able to:

- work with co-ordinates and draw graphs;

- understand patterns in multiplication and addition;

- talk about patterns;

- use simple formulae and equations; and

- use the relationship between multiplication and division.

Algebra is not about letters! It is the use of patterns and relationships to make general rules from which you can work out answers to particular problems. To do this Alik needs to have the opportunity to work on real problems and to explain through talk his strategies and approaches. He needs to be able to manipulate sets of numbers in order to explore patterns and relationships.

Measures Tom is nine and is working at Level 3 in all of his mathematics work. It is important to realise that children can be on different Levels in the different areas of mathematics. You may have memories of yourself or your friends saying such things as 'I like algebra but I don't understand geometry'. It is the same for our children. Tom is expected to:

- be familiar with and be using a range of metric units;

- select the right sorts of measuring tools for a given task;

- tell the time on all kinds of clocks;

- be able to read instruments such as a speedometer; and

- be able to make sensible estimates of size, length and so on.

In order to acquire these skills and understandings Tom has had to use tapes, rulers and measuring wheels to measure, for example, the playground, the hall or the sizes of books. He has learned to tell the time and understands the relationship between a scale and a pointer along that scale. he can weigh things and can talk sensibly about the sizes of things. He will only acquire and continue to develop his understanding of measures and measurement through a combination of practical activity, talk and recording.

Shape and space Sally is five and is getting to grips with Level 1. In order to do this she is working in a very practical way with a wide variety of familiar objects. Sally is starting to develop her mathematics from her real world. It is important to keep in mind that mathematics is a tool which has been developed over the centuries out of real situations and happenings. The need for practical activity does not stop as we grow older. In order for Sally to progress through Level 1 she must have the opportunity to learn to:

- sort collections of objects in respect of shape and size;

- make three-dimensional models;

- draw shapes and describe them;

- use words such as 'inside' and 'next to' appropriately; and
- move to given instructions.

By the end of her primary education Sally should be operating with a full knowledge of angles, patterns, symmetry and rotation in both two and three dimensions. Her work at Level 1 is the solid foundation for a more sophisticated understanding of shape and space. Sally must not be pushed through the early Levels too quickly in order to get to Levels where she must do more pencil and paper work. The handling of real objects is essential to her development.

Data handling Carmen is eight and is working with Level 3 material. She has already experienced a lot of practical work to do with sorting and classifying things and can use and produce block graphs. She is also aware of probability in the sense that she appreciates that some events or happenings are more likely than others. In working at Level 3 she is now able to:

- organise information about herself;
- read off information in such things as catalogues;
- construct bar charts; and
- predict the likelihood of certain events, for example, in rolling a die or tossing a coin.

We are all surrounded by information and we all make decisions based on our interpretations of bits of that information. For example, whether we are considering which new toaster to buy or looking at the interest rates on savings accounts or even deciding whether to have a day out on the basis of a weather forecast, we are handling data and weighing probabilities. Carmen is now well on the road to being able to make sensible decisions and through these decisions to increase her control over her own life.

School maths may still look fairly intimidating to us parents, and we may feel that, even though our children are young, they have already learned more than us in mathematics. It is a problem, then, to know how best to help them. There is some advice about how to help your children in Chapter 4. It is enough to say here that it is probably not a good idea to try to reinterpret what they are doing in the light of what you know, but to engage them in looking at the maths problems you have to solve in real life. At the very least they will learn that maths is essential and useful, and that maths is about problems which often have more than one solution. Maths is not just sums!

THE CORE SUBJECTS: SCIENCE

Systematic methods rigorously applied

Scientists commonly use a number of skills in trying to find out about things and to solve problems. These skills, which include close observation, logical thinking and carefully set out results, have come to be known as scientific method. The National Curriculum for science ensures that children have a chance to learn these skills, as well as learning facts. Science is not set out, though, under the headings many of us can remember, that is physics, chemistry and biology. Rather, the approach is through broad sectors of scientific knowledge such as 'Forces' 'Sound and music'. Each of these sectors is an Attainment Target and there are seventeen of them in the science programme. Of these seventeen Attainment Targets not all are designed for use with children in primary schools. The range for these children is ATs 1–6 and 9–16.

Attainment Target 1 is all about scientific method, and is officially labelled 'Exploration of science, communication and the application of knowledge and understanding'. All the other Targets contain scientific knowledge and are labelled 'Knowledge and understanding of science, communication, and the applications and implications of science'. (*Science in the National Curriculum.* (1989) DES and the Welsh Office, p. iii.)

This overall title does not tell us exactly what school science is about, and unlike the mathematics programme it is not so easy to simplify the set of Attainment Targets. They can be grouped in a variety of ways. One way of grouping them which may make them easier to understand is as follows:

All about life	The variety of life, life processes, genetics and evolution, life and energy (ATs 2, 3, 4 and parts of 13).
Our Earth	Our effects on the Earth, all about materials found on Earth, Earth and atmosphere, Earth in space (ATs 5, 6, 9 and 16).
Forces and energy	Forces, electricity and magnetism, information transfer and microelectronics, energy sources, transfer and control, sound and music, light and electromagnetism (ATs 10, 11, 12, parts of 13, 14 and 15).

All of these Attainment Targets are supported by AT 1 which is about the methods of science and therefore runs through all scientific work.

What this means for science lessons

Because you cannot learn a way of doing something without actually doing it, teachers will try to get children learning the scientific facts by using all the aspects of scientific method that they also need to learn. If you put scientific method together with scientific fact, the approach to learning that comes through is a problem-solving approach. Children should therefore be finding out or testing the facts through practical activity. We have deliberately not used the word 'experiment', because this conjures up rascally attempts to blow up the school. Children will indeed be doing experiments, but they will involve using a much wider range of everyday things and not the bunsen burners and flasks filled with bubbling concoctions that we may associate with school science. Putting science at the heart of the curriculum for young children has a big effect on what they spend their time doing in school. Our own infant and junior schooldays did not commonly present us with experimental challenge and related practical activity.

It is ironic that our lack of early work in science may have contributed to the shortage of teachers with scientific skills and qualifications now. There will be attempts through the training of teachers outside their working day, to give them the skills to help the children. Teachers need as much support, help and encouragement as the children to develop their science. The list of things children should have the chance to learn makes the science curriculum seem very complex. There is indeed much work to do, and it is up to individual teachers and schools as to how they tackle it. They may look for science themes which take in work to meet several Attainment Targets. They may do some science as part of a broad topic like 'food' or 'hot and cold', or they may tackle one Attainment Target at a time. As the children progress through the Levels, it may be necessary to do more learning at 'secondhand', that is from books and the results of other people's experiments. The National Curriculum for science makes it clear, though, that the emphasis should be, where possible, on first-hand practical activity.

We will now look at some typical children who are at various stages of their scientific education, and describe the kinds of things they may be learning in school.

Work at Level 3 in a science theme Cheryl is in a 'mixed-age' lower junior class, sometimes called 'vertically grouped' or 'family grouped'. There are seven-, eight- and nine-year-olds in her class. The teacher is, of course, providing each child with work that is appropriate for him/her. The whole class has been engaged in a 'Life science' theme, and Cheryl, aged eight, is working with five other children all at Level 3. In terms of scientific method (AT 1) the teacher is checking that Cheryl's group all get a chance to:

- set up ideas for testing;

- do experiments over time, and look for change;

- know what a fair test is;

- use instruments like magnifiers;

- measure variables with simple instruments;

- record results on various kinds of charts;

- interpret simple charts;

- review results and come to a general final statement; and

- put activities into a sequence.

They may, of course, not all get the chance to learn to do all of these things during the current theme, but their teacher will be constantly monitoring her own teaching and their learning to ensure they all eventually get that chance.

Now to the facts. Cheryl and her workmates, through a variety of practical activities and through reading and writing, will be learning the following concepts:

- there are similarities and differences among living things;

- living things can be put in groups according to features we can see;

- living things react to seasonal and daily changes;

- life processes are found in people and other creatures; and
- the steps in the human life cycle.

They may be growing plants, pond-dipping, examining minibeasts, observing their pets, visiting a farm or zoo, and recording information about themselves and their families. All of these activities will be set up, with the teacher's help and questioning, to satisfy the rigour of scientific experimentation. There may, however, be occasions when the children can devise their own experiments.

While Cheryl is working on Level 3 activities, there will be other children or groups of children in the class working at Level 2, and Level 4. The activities they will be required to do will differ, though they will be able to use some of the same things to do their experiments.

Work at Level 5 in linear fashion Clive is an extremely able eleven-year-old in a top junior class. He is the only child in the class to be working through Level 5 across the whole science curriculum. The teacher has devised an individual science work programme for him. He is given an assignment within one of the Attainment Targets. He completes a list of things he wants to find out, decides on an order in which to tackle them, and sets down in rough an experimental design. When the teacher has seen his planned work, he collects the things he needs for the experiment, sets it up, records the results and pursues the enquiry or takes up another problem from his list.

From Attainment Target 1, here are the aspects of scientific method that the teacher must ensure he has the chance to learn:

- use what he knows to suggest research problems and design experiments to solve them (he can do this already);

- know what to do with dependent and independent variables;

- select and use appropriate measuring instruments; and

- derive patterns from data from various sources and record them.

His current assignment meets Attainment Target 15 which says that he should understand how light is reflected. At other Levels he has done experiments with, for example, mirrors and shadows and he knows light travels in straight lines. In designing experiments at his present Level he will be drawing on, for example, his knowledge of angles, and his discoveries about reflectors in headlamps and torches, the shape of the surface of mirrors used for shaving and the operation of a periscope.

Level 1 across the curriculum Darren has been at school for one term and has just turned five. He is in a reception class of four- and five-year-olds. Though children aged four are not required to study the National Curriculum, the teacher does give even the youngest children a chance to join in all the activities. She has a number of activities going on at the same time in the room. In a typical morning, Darren will have the chance to do work contributing to his science education in the following ways:

- take a good look at the seashell display in the hallway, and drop some into the see-through water tank on display to see what happens (AT 1, AT 6 and AT 15);

- talk about the weather and what he saw on the way to school (AT 1 and AT 9); and

- feed the school budgie and draw a picture of him from life and talk to the teacher about the parts of the bird in the picture (AT 1, AT 2 and AT 3).

That is by no means all that Darren will do in a morning. Clearly his work needs extending and the teacher will help, by her questioning, to make his observations systematic. But he is making a start on science.

WHAT ELSE IS TO BE TAUGHT?

Now that we know what the core curriculum looks like, we know that teachers will have to work up a smart juggling act to allow enough lesson time to be spent on the other subjects (that is the other Foundation subjects) set out in the National Curriculum. While a big proportion of the school day may be labelled English, mathematics and science; technology, history, geography, music, art, physical education and religious education have to be fitted in too. The documents relating to some of these subjects have yet to be published. Their introduction into schools is to be phased. At the earliest, it will not be until the Autumn term 1992 that the full National Curriculum is in place in primary schools. In the meantime, teachers may focus on the subjects where they do have documentation and other subjects may get less time than they should in the school day. The reasons for this are understandable. Teachers are human and will focus on what they know rather than anticipate what they do not, and they want to fully understand and work the

Core subjects, before juggling the others too. One way of starting to understand how our children's schools are handling the balance of activities and offering our children a broad and balanced curriculum is to find out about class timetables.

TIMETABLES

All teachers operate timetables. There are enormous variations between different teachers and different schools. There is also a huge number of factors for teacher to accommodate in timetabling. As a schoolchild or a parent, these things may not be self-evident. They include items like:

- What are the fixed points in the schoolday? (For example, is assembly always at the same time, does the class have the hall for gymnastics or dance at a fixed time?)

- Is the classroom put to other uses? (For example, are dinners eaten in there, or is there a computer club which demands desks empty of workbooks?)

- Is there a whole school timetable and what limits does that place on the class?

- Are some of the things the children need for their learning in another part of the school (for example computers) and can they be brought to the children or do the children have to go to them?

- What are the shared resources, and how can the teacher work out when it is her turn to have them?

- When is there quiet and when is there noise in the schoolday? (For example, from the kitchen, other classes, the traffic or the factory next door.)

- What is the teacher like and what is her preferred style of working?

- What are the children like and how is school time best structured to fit their needs.

With all these things in mind, each teacher tries to work out a form of timetabling which matches her own teaching style and the needs of her class. Some teachers prefer to be more 'old-fashioned', didactic and formal. Others choose a 'progressive' informal approach. Most real teachers fall somewhere in between, and assume one or the other style, according to the circumstances, group of children and particular teaching point. Appearances can be deceptive, though. It is tempting to think that the teacher who runs several activities at a time, or encourages the children to leave their desks in the course of their work is the one who is easy-going about timetables, but that may not be so.

We can imagine a class in which all the children do a certain kind of English work every Friday afternoon. If the rest of the week is predetermined like that, then the timetable is so easy to construct and carry through that neither teacher nor children need it after a week or two.

In another class, the children work sometimes in groups and sometimes individually, and the children assigned to different groups vary according to the activity. The children have some flexibility about the order in which they tackle the tasks for the day. There are opportunities for children to carry their own learning as far as they can, even if the work continues into another session. In this class, the teacher may not draw all the children together, let alone their work, from one end of the day to the other. Clearly there is not one timetable operating here, but as many timetables as there are children, and probably one for the teacher too. This vision can be so different from our own idea of school, that we think it may be chaotic. However, if the intention in school is to teach children how to study, in which class would we find more independent learners? These two classrooms are hypothetical, and most actual classes have a bit of both about them. There is little doubt that to be effective, both kinds of teachers need considerable management skills.

Whatever the kind of timetable the teacher operates, the really important issue is the way the teacher and the children manage their time. Give your children help with ways to use time well, and it gives them more chance to learn. (There's more advice on children and time management in Chapter 4.) The child who takes ten minutes longer than the others to get what he needs for his work, will probably not do as much or as well as some of the other children.

People in education often talk about 'good practice'. When it comes to timetables, there are no rules about what is 'good'. However, it is definitely not good if a timetable is made to operate at the expense of children's learning, or teacher's teaching. For the children, a good timetable is one which enables every child (maybe not all the time) to carry their learning forward beyond the lesson allocation, and finish off work while it is fresh.

LEARNING ACROSS THE SCHOOL

One of the constant problems teachers have to face is how to provide learning opportunities appropriate for every child. Because the National Curriculum means that teachers must give children work at the Levels appropriate for them, some teachers may have to change their way of working. Though the teacher can introduce a topic to the whole class, she can no longer teach, for example, a science lesson to a class where individual children are known to be working at Levels 2, 3, 4 or 5 (and this range is quite possible in a class near the top of the junior school). Work at these Levels is different, both in content and to some extent in the way it must be presented. You should expect children in the same class as your child to sometimes be doing different work.

Schools may start to solve the problem of matching Level

of work to child in a number of ways. One of these is to make the children more 'mobile' and have, for example, the Level 3 science going on at one time and in one room in the school. As parents, we do not really like this idea. It is okay if your child is seven and feels good about working with ten-year-olds, but it is not so good if you happen to have a ten-year-old who is placed amongst infants for science. Another way of handling this problem is to have the infant department operate as a team and provide the range of learning opportunities required. The junior department can then operate as a similar team.

TOPICS

Topics, projects and themes have been common in primary schools for some time. If your children are in schools where topics have not been a regular feature, then there may be more in future. Typically, topics have a 'big' title, under which teaching and learning in a number of subjects can take place.

A whole curriculum topic For example, the teacher may choose a topic title which is directly related to work which has gone on in schools, even before the National Curriculum came into force. 'Homes' is one such title, and under this heading there may be work in:

- English (all the spoken and written work, whether descriptions of real homes, stories or poetry);

- mathematics (counting, measuring, estimating);

- science (structures, building materials, weathering);

- history (architecture, lifestyle);

- geography (homes around the world);

- art (drawing the homes near school, inventing homes of the future, design within the home);

- PE (dance drama with house-building or 'The Three Pigs' as a theme); and

- religious education (the parable of the man who built his house upon the rock . . . or the story of Noah).

The possibilities are legion.

As you can see, the topic above does allow the possibility of work across many subjects. One of the benefits of topics is that the limits to the work 'allowed' are set by the learners, that is the teacher and children, rather than the subject matter.

Topic focus decided by teacher The teacher may wish to focus on study methods rather than content and, for example, in a topic named 'Stormy Weather', she may get the children to make systematic weather reports and look with them at methods of reporting. The children may also work out ways of getting information and compiling a log through finding out the effects of wild weather on the lives of the dinner ladies. The resulting work would arm the children with methods they might use in another enquiry. If that same teacher was going for an 'across all the subjects approach', she would, for example, get the children to listen to 'stormy' music, write 'stormy' poetry, enact a shipwreck in dance drama and listen to the 'stormy' passages in, for example, *Robinson Crusoe* and other classic accounts. They may also learn the names of cloud formations or how and why storms occur, and measure the wind and rainfall.

Topic work decided by children Under any topic heading the teacher can consult with the children about what they want to know. This approach is particularly useful with:

- topics about the children themselves (for example health education); and

- topics set up for individual children.

If, for example, the teacher is working with her class on 'Feet', she will want them to find out the association between feet and measurement; whether they can record foot sizes for the class on a graph; whether foot size is related to height; shoe fashions; whether there are differences between people in terms of footedness; and the materials and processes in shoe manufacture. She will also want them to learn about foot care and will be guided by their questions in devising their work programme.

Of course, however teachers approach topic work, they will now have to check that the work done as a topic ties in with that necessary in the National Curriculum. The topic may exceed the work necessary, but the National Curriculum tells teachers the minimum they must do.

WHAT TEACHERS AND CHILDREN DO IN LESSONS

When people are asked to picture a teacher at work, there are a variety of images that come to mind. Some people see an austere figure standing in front of a class and speaking to them in a loud and commanding voice while silent children sit at individual desks. They may see that same teacher writing assiduously on the blackboard, while the children, equally assiduously copy down. Others will see a much more accessible person who spends much of her time kneeling on the floor with the counting blocks, or sitting on a child-size chair alongside a group of working children.

For us, it may be that the image is part of our own memory of schooldays. It is possible that we get our ideas about teachers from other sources too. These may include films, TV and books. Even small children operate stereotypes when they 'play' school. They demand rapt attention from all their pupils. They totally control the situation and they are very harsh disciplinarians. Stereotypes, though, are unreal for they do not give a whole picture. It may be that some teachers, in some lessons, in some schools still fit the image of a rather distant authority figure. Victorian architecture, very old furniture and over-large classes, can affect the options teachers have about ways of working.

It is more common nowadays for classrooms to have a group-based seating plan, with more opportunity for children to talk to each other, and space for the teacher to gather all the children together when necessary and to move about the room talking with groups or individual children for some of the time. In lesson time, the teacher talks to the class, a group or individuals. She may work with a group or individual child, encouraging their thinking by appropriate questioning, or she may observe or assess a child who is at work. Marking work with children may be an opportunity to encourage and help them. This picture of the teacher is a very long way from some of our images of the teacher. It is a picture of an adult enabling, encouraging and helping children to learn. In contrast, our mental image is of the all-knowing adult telling us all that we have to memorise.

Which do we prefer for our children? There is something to be said for 'knowing where you are' and we certainly knew exactly what was expected of us when we had to listen to the teacher nearly all day. These days there is no sure way of knowing what children have done in school. There is also the expectation that they will, even at a young age, be more self-determining and self-motivating. The real question is whether what they experience in school matches what they need for life in the next century.

SUMMARY

We have looked at how the National Curriculum imperatives change lessons in the Core subjects. If we look now at a general picture of what children do in lessons, an enormous list of things can be compiled. Individual children's experience will vary according to their teachers and schools. Commonly, we can expect our children to do talking, listening, and to share ideas. They read from a variety of books, learn to look things up, and write in a range of ways for different purposes. They fetch what they need for their own learning, and do practical work to find things out and solve problems. They sit still sometimes, and move about the room and the school in the course of their learning. They should be guided in all this by some basic principles describing what education is. Their teachers should be able to tell you what these ideas are, and where the ideas come from. In the next Chapter there is discussion about finding out how your children are getting on.

— 3 —

HOW IS MY CHILD DOING?

SOURCES OF INFORMATION

There are four main ways of finding out how our children are progressing at school. These are:

- reading the reports and results of tests they bring home;

- looking for clues in the work they bring home, such as the teacher's comments, and the kind of book they have as a home reader;

- going into school and asking the classteacher and looking at work there; and

- asking the children themselves.

These are not placed in order of their real importance, but in the order that we, as parents, often try to establish progress in school. If we turned the list upside down it may better reflect the important things first. Because we are busy people, and are not sure how to interpret the things our children and sometimes their teachers tell us about how they are working, we go for tangible written evidence of performance in school.

Each of these ways need to be explored for each provides slightly different kinds of information and each is only a partial view. We shall start with test results and reports as these are much changed by the National Curriculum.

TESTS: WHEN THEY WILL BE SET AND WHAT THEY WILL BE LIKE

National tests

An important part of the Education Reform Act is that which sets out assessment arrangements for the National Curriculum. The plans for assessment embrace a whole range of ways in which our children will undertake assessment tasks. These include oral and practical tests, projects and written tests. It is intended that continuous assessment by teachers will be part of the assessment package. There will also be a number of external tests devised and set for use in State schools throughout England and Wales. These are called 'Standard Assessment Tasks' (SATs), and are the tests which children will do at the end of each Key Stage. Teachers in some schools tried out a variety of the things that may be put in the tests during the 1989–90 school year.

When tests will take place

Under the National Curriculum, children must do special tests at the end of each Key Stage. Teachers are advised that the end of a Key Stage is reached when the majority of children in the class are aged seven or eleven. But in some small primary schools, where mixed-age classes are common, it may be that each child is said to reach the end of a Key Stage towards the end of the school year in which they become seven or eleven. However the school decides to give Key Stage assessments, the needs of our children will be paramount and the Education Reform Act makes this clear. Schools will not be able to vary or amalgamate the Key Stages. This will, of course, produce some difficulties for those areas which have Middle schools, where the age-range is eight to twelve or nine to thirteen. Those of you who have children at such schools will need to take an active interest in how your local education authority is responding to the linking of Key Stage 1 to the age of seven and Key Stage 2 to the age of eleven. But it is important to keep in mind that the Key Stages are assessment points and not end points for the Levels in Attainment Targets.

Tests for seven-year-olds The school year 1990–91 is the first year when seven-year-olds will have studied the National Curriculum for Key Stage 1, and so these children are being tested in every school across England and Wales. This is a full 'trial run' and the results will not be reported to us, the parents. Instead, the results will be compared by teachers from different schools, to ensure that they are operating the same standards. In 1991–92 and thereafter, the results of the SATs carried out by seven-year-olds will come to parents.

Tests for eleven-year-olds Because the National Curriculum is being introduced in a phased way, the first 'trial run' for eleven-year-olds comes in 1991–92. As is happening with the first tests taken by seven-year-olds, the results of these first tests will not be reported to parents, but will be used for moderation.

Reporting test results and teacher assessments to parents

Classteachers and schools may give parents a whole range of information about their children's progress at various points throughout their primary years. The points at which they must now, by law, report to parents are at age seven and eleven. These ages may be referred to as a 'reporting ages'. The aggregate results of the SATs for all the children who took them in each school may be made public for both age groups. Headteachers are, however, by law obliged to make public only the results of SATs done at age eleven. We should note that our individual children's results are confidential, between ourselves, our children and their teachers.

How children will be tested

There are many important considerations that the people devising the tests need to take into account. These include things like: how to test the way the children tackle practical activities and problem solving; how to test children whose recording skills are not extensive; and how to test communication skills, including speaking and listening. Some elements of traditional tests (commonly called pencil and paper) have been abandoned in favour of test tasks which children do in groups. The teacher observes the way the children tackle the task, and asks questions about what they are doing and what they plan to do, in order to find out their level of understanding. There is often some writing or drawing to be done in these tasks too. Some assessments need to be made by the teacher while the work is going on, whilst some can be made on the basis of what the children have written down.

These ways of testing children's performance sound very complicated, and so they are. Testing human beings is an

almost impossible business because our knowledge and skills are so complex, and we always use a whole batch of concepts and abilities in tackling any one thing. There are also theoretical principles which people writing the tests have to consider. These include whether the test actually gets at what you want to measure (then it is a valid test) and whether it is more important to know how well someone does when compared with thousands of other similar people or how well someone does when measured against the task itself. If we look at an example of each of these kinds of test it is easier to see their strengths and weaknesses.

Norm- and criterion-referenced tests Intelligence tests are norm-referenced tests. They have been worked out, tested and re-tested on large numbers of people. Most people get a score somewhere near the middle of the possible range of scores. As you go further from the middle, fewer and fewer people get very 'low' or very 'high' scores. For any individual, you can see where they fit in relation to most other people, that is against the 'norm'.

The second kind of test is more like a driving test. You learn the skills and concepts necessary. You take the test and you pass. You are not being matched against other people's performance, but against whether you can do a three-point turn or whatever. These sorts of tests are criterion-referenced; that is, you are tested against predetermined criteria and it does not matter how many of us pass. In fact the expectation is that you take the test when you are ready to pass.

The official tests for the National Curriculum combine some of the elements of both kinds of test. The tests are tasks against which the children are matched, but on the basis of that performance the teacher will assess at what Level the child is working, which involves some elements of comparison with other children, especially when these results are put alongside those of a nationwide sample. Tests are still being designed and it will be some time before the full array of possible tests is available to us. However, it is possible to indicate the sorts of tasks that our children will encounter.

Integrated tests A typical situation will be where a group of children, say five or six, are given a set of tasks which relate to a particular topic. An example might look like this:

Topic: Buried treasure.

Aim: The children must attempt to locate some buried treasure using a variety of clues.

Resources: Map, paper, craft materials e.g. sticky tape, straws, card and scissors, clues which could be based on books they know, ideas in mathematics and so on.

Tasks: Working together the children will have to:
- interpret clues;
- be able to read maps;
- explain and agree decisions;
- construct models e.g. simple crane; and
- write a story on and/or keep a log of their expedition.

In undertaking this sort of test children will be demonstrating work in English (speaking and listening, reading, writing and associated skills); mathematics (co-ordinates, measuring, solving clues); geography (maps and map-reading); technology and design (model construction); as well as a range of inter-personal skills. Their teacher will have to observe the children in order to assess their spoken work and the quality of individual contributions. She will be able to assess their written work away from the task.

Subject tests Within subjects there are groups of concepts and ideas which children need to learn in order to get an overall grasp of the subject. Each group of ideas is called an Attainment Target. Subject tests have to address the Attainment Targets. However, at present there do not seem to be national plans to set subject specific tests for children in primary schools. Whilst there will be teachers who will assess progress in particular Attainment Targets at the appropriate Levels throughout the school year, the Key Stage assessments are likely to embrace larger units of work. This reinforces a thematic or topic approach to SATs.

Local tests Many schools have used tests they have 'bought in' rather than devised themselves, even before the advent of the National Curriculum. Headteachers may still want to continue to do these kinds of test in addition to those required by law. Local education authorities may also suggest that schools in their areas do tests at other times as well as those at the end of each Key Stage.

TEACHER ASSESSMENTS

The advisers on assessment in the National Curriculum have emphasised the importance of assessments made by teachers throughout the school year. These are commonly called 'continuous assessment'. They are seen as making a major contribution to an overall picture of children's performance. Anyone who has ever done an exam will know that things you knew and could do perfectly the week before the exam, somehow do not come right when you are actually doing the test. Some people are much better at doing tests than others. It is quite appropriate that the teacher who has seen Owen and Claire in action all year should be able to add her judgements to the results that Owen and Claire obtain in SATs.

Parents and children are concerned that tests, and their marking and interpretation, should be fair. Some children do not get along with their teacher, and it is this same teacher who will be responsible for continually making judgements about performance. Whilst the vast majority of teachers do their utmost to be fair to all the children in their care, there will be a few who allow personality clashes to influence their judgements. It is in the best interests of children, parents and teachers, to use a system which supports monitoring of both teacher assessments and nationally-set tests.

There are three major steps which are being introduced in order for us all to feel comfortable with the assessment of our childrens' learning. These are:

- the introduction of annual meetings of governors and parents where issues can be aired;

- reporting to parents; and

- the moderation of teachers' assessments by others from outside the school.

What happens in the moderation process is that teachers from a group of schools get together and compare their assessments to make sure they are operating the same standards. These meetings will take place regularly. Moderation is a familiar process in secondary schools in relation to GCSE and has been a full part of college, polytechnic and university assessments for many years. However, external moderation is new in the primary school and there will be a period of training and trialling to be undertaken.

REPORTS

The broad range of information being made available to parents will include official test results and teacher assessments about our children. Schools may also make it possible for teachers to comment on work in areas other than the Foundation subjects, and to say what study and social skills each child has developed. If we look at a number of typical children, at various stages in their primary school career, we can see what may be reported to their parents.

A reception year report

Paul is at the end of his first year in school. Towards the end of the summer term, his parents were invited to go and see his classteacher in an informal setting. When they went along, they were able to look around the school and classroom, at the displays of children's work and at Paul's work in his books. They then talked to his teacher about how he had settled into school and his performance in speaking and listening, reading, writing, maths and science. The teacher pointed out to them on a report form, that Paul is working towards Level 1 across the curriculum. He talks freely to the teacher and his vocabulary and articulation are good. His reading skills arc not yet developed, and he is working on picture and caption books. He is also making little books, using his own words, which he then reads and re-reads. The teacher says that his skills in writing will go alongside reading. In maths he has been working on counting, matching and pattern-making, and has tried some measuring and shape work. In science his teacher has been helping him to really look at things, and talk about and draw what he sees. His teacher says he is keen and interested, and eager to learn. The teacher also pointed out that she had written on the report form the kinds of work Paul is doing in the other subjects, that is technology, history, geography, art, music and PE. In her final comments, the teacher mentioned the RE work of the class, and the indications about Paul's social development, including whether he likes taking on little jobs and whether he works and plays cooperatively for some of the time. The teacher then gave Paul's parents a copy of the report for their own record. The teacher's copy was added to the school records.

An end of Key Stage 1 report

Debbie is seven and has just completed her top infant year. In the language of the National Curriculum, she is at the end of Key Stage 1. She has done SATs during the summer term. The SATs covered some aspects of the Core subjects, English, maths and science. Her parents were invited to see her teacher. Her teacher told them how Debbie had worked over the whole year (all of her comments being based on her continuous assessment) and told them of Debbie's performance in the SATs, compared with the teacher's own expectations and with the performance of her classmates. She did not mention other children by name, but indicated in general whether Debbie was doing as well as other children of her age. Debbie's parents were given a report which included the teacher's comments on Debbie's work in each aspect of the curriculum throughout the year (including the Levels at which she is working), the results of the SATs, and the starter page of a 'Profile' of Debbie's skills and development. Among the things it said, the profile indicated that Debbie is thoughtful and articulate and sympathetic to the views of other people. These are skills she can build on. The profile also said that Debbie has difficulties in maths, particularly in aspects of maths involving spatial skills. This indicates an area where Debbie may need extra help in school in future.

From the examples of Paul and Debbie, we can see that the reports can be cumulative and increase in coverage as children go up the school.

A second year junior report

Robert, aged nine, has a folder of reports and teachers' written comments at home, and now, at the end of his second year in the juniors, the classteacher has again had the opportunity to discuss his work with his parents, and to point out

to them the strengths on which he can build and the areas in which he needs to have more support. His report extends to Levels reached in the subjects of the National Curriculum, work done in other areas, and a profile of aspects of his development.

An end of Key Stage 2 report

For Adam, aged eleven, the report and teacher comments he has just received are very important as he has reached the end of Key Stage 2. Adam has just finished his primary education, and a copy of the teacher's report and comments have gone to his new school. The full dossier, which his parents have had a chance to read, includes a detailed profile of his development from his early years, a summary of the work he has covered in the Foundation subjects and the Levels he has reached. Some samples of his work are included to indicate his recent progress.

The actual appearance of the report on each child may vary from one school to another or from one area to another. As the kinds of assessment under the National Curriculum become refined there may be some central recommendations about the style of the reporting. What is more likely, is that local authorities will devise a report form for use in their schools, as they have in the past. However, as the minimum content of the curriculum is now uniform, the differences from one authority to another should not be great. Indeed, one of the major purposes of the National Curriculum is to support compatability between schools and local education authorities.

Reports may contain the mention of **Profile Components**. This label is given to a cluster of Attainment Targets which have been grouped for reporting purposes. For example, in English, the Profile Component 'Writing' comprises writing (content), handwriting and spelling.

POSSIBLE CONSEQUENCES OF NATIONAL CURRICULUM ASSESSMENT

Testing

The possible trend to increased testing may be encouraging to some people. A number of parents are keen to have 'marks' attached to the intellectual performance of their children. This is often associated with a desire for their children to develop a determination to be competitive in what is seen as being a competitive world. However, there are some disadvantages to an increase in tests. It does make some teachers worry more about tests than teaching, and teaching, after all, is not only about telling children how to do tests! It does make some children worry about 'marks' rather than learning. It can also have the effect of making us think about narrow linear learning rather than the development of alternative solutions and creative answers. Children do have to learn how to do exams, but exams are not at the heart of education. Education is about personal enrichment for life, and you can actually get the discipline for that without passing exams. The fact that the proposed national tests will often operate in the context of groups of children should help in maintaining that proper balance between competition and fruitful cooperation. But to do so, this system will need the support of all parents.

Reporting

The problems of compiling reports that comply with National Curriculum assessment have not yet fully come to light. Primary teachers do see the whole business of assessment as an extra burden on them. Reports to parents may, therefore, not be as comprehensive as we parents might wish. However, it is important that we neither ignore nor set too much store by reports. On the one hand reports do give us another perspective on our children's progress and achievements, and one that comes from outside the home. On the other, they can contain very cryptic information which can cause misunderstandings and, at times, heartache. What our son or daughter has learned in a year cannot be summarised by a row of ticks in boxes, and reports like this are clearly woefully inadequate. Reports containing general statements which are open to a variety of interpretations are also of little real use. Fortunately, most teachers do try to communicate the essential information to us, and to future teachers of our children. There is very rarely any intent to cast a blight on our children.

In reacting to reports we feel it is a good idea to look at style and format. So check your child's report against the following questions before you embark on any discussion.

- Does the report list things only by subject? If it does, ask whether topics and other cross-curricular work is taken into account.

- Is there space for full comments? If not, ask the class-teacher to find out why the space is limited and whether it can be extended.

- Is there space for you to write a response? If not, ask if a space can be included on the next report you see, and if you wish, attach your comments to the report.

- Does the report allow you to understand your child's progress as well as achievement? If not, ask about progress and see if indications of progress can be entered in.

- Does the report indicate aptitudes and include a comment on social and personal development? If not, do ask if it can be added.

- What provision is made to discuss the report? If there is none, and you would like to discuss it, make an appointment with the classteacher, and go and talk it over.

Reports are confidential, but they are transmitted from teacher to teacher. It is, therefore, vital that all parties are clear about what they mean and agree on their contents – and that includes your son or daughter.

The publication of results

It is difficult to predict what the publication of results will do to or for schools. If local education authorities compile league tables of their schools' aggregate results in each subject then there is a clear possibility that some schools will be more highly regarded than others on the basis of those results. This might mean that more parents will choose to try and send their children to one particular school, and difficulties may occur if this happens. You may like a school, and your child may be happy there, but you might feel under pressure to move him if the average 'results' are not as good as the school down the road. Schools do not have the opportunity for infinite growth and some parents and their children will be turned away. Averaging results of SATs will blur the possibilities that your child has for individual achievement. It is not the case that better scores necessarily mean better

teaching and learning. The children at a particular school may enter with more basic skills at the outset, or may get coaching for the tests. What we, as parents, need to establish is likely to be only partly supported by the publication of SATs. The important things should be to do with our child's growth physically, emotionally and intellectually. We are in many ways best placed to appreciate how our sons or daughters are maturing in their approach to life, including their schooling. Although there may be many pressures for us to move our children from one school to another, these should be resisted unless we are certain that a move is totally in the interests of our children and not because we are over-rating the status of test results.

On the other hand, there are now clear requirements for schools to make a full range of information and views available to us. On the basis of this information we should be able to take a much more balanced view of schooling than we may have been able to do up to the present time. Much of the 'secret garden' of education is now open to public view and opinion.

As well as the official indications of how well our children are getting on, we parents also try to make judgements about the work they bring home. We shall look at this next.

POINTERS TO PROGRESS: WORK CHILDREN BRING HOME

Reading books

English is at the heart of the primary school curriculum and reading has become the most common measure we use for how well our children are getting on in their intellectual development. We also have ready access to it. We can see if they look at the newspaper or sauce bottle, or look at the advertising hoardings and read comics. However, because it is easier to tell how our children are reading, this is often one of the things we worry about. The amount of interest is not entirely unfounded, because reading is a skill they need in all the other subjects and in much of the learning done outside school too. We do say more about offering a 'reading environment' at home in Chapter 4.

It may be helpful here to give some pointers to the way teachers are teaching reading nowadays. It is actually not known how children learn to read; it is a complex business (like all human learning). What teachers do, is to first show interest and enjoyment when reading themselves. They read to the children regularly, so that some of their interest and enjoyment will infect the children. Teachers also try to make books tempting by displaying them attractively, pointing them out to the children and, where possible, creating areas in the school and classroom where children can read comfortably. Then they help children to gain all the skills that 'good' readers have. They help them discriminate between the shapes we call letters, show them that we look at a page from left to right, starting at the top. They help them to look for clues in the pictures about what the writing says and anticipate what the next word or bit of the story might be. They help them to memorise words they are going to need a lot by labelling things and putting captions under pictures. The final thing that teachers do is try to make opportunities for children to look at books, read books and use books. Some teachers make use of reading schemes to support a number of these activities, but reading schemes are only as good as the teacher makes them. There is sometimes an over pre-occupation with schemes, and schemes do not teach reading, they are only one part of our children's experience.

If you picture all these things going on in schools, then it does make us feel a bit less anxious about whether our own son or daughter has actually read aloud from their reading book to an adult each day in school.

Topic work

It is difficult to know how your children are getting on in topic or project work. Some of us have children who give us a blow-by-blow account of their day. Others of us have children who lead another life at school and never say a word about their work. Even when your son or daughter does tell you all, it is not often that they tell you the detailed sequence of how a piece of work is developing or why they have to collect ten matchboxes for Monday. But there are opportunities to get to know the outcomes of project work. Children sometimes bring such work home, and project work is often displayed at open evenings. Months or even years later our children suddenly make new connections and manage total recall . . . 'Mum, we did a topic on that in Miss Jones' class and the best bit was when . . .' The most important reaction that we must have to topic work is to appreciate that it involves 'proper' work. It is tempting to see topics or projects as somehow being easier and therefore less important than other things. What may actually be the case is that a topic is highly motivating and children learn more readily. They also get the chance to make connections between ideas across subjects. This is creative thinking. The National Curriculum statements and intentions make clear that well-organised topic work will be an essential part of the learning opportunities provided for all of our children.

Workbooks

Reading books and project work are often brought home by children. They may also bring home a whole bundle of work at the end of a year or Key Stage. It is useful to have a look at it and compare it with the last lot you had (which may have been the year before). Then choose something representative or entertaining (children's 'news' books can provide a wonderful record of family events and mishaps) and keep it for your children to look at when they are grown up. While there should be some signs of development over the years, remember that what is written down is not a complete or even representative record of intellectual development.

Artwork

We associate art with 'free expression' and sometimes assume that it can be a 'time-filler' in school. This is simply not correct. There is as much discipline and there are at least as many skills involved in drawing a picture of the person you sit next to as there is in conducting an experiment or writing a story. Any teacher who puts art at the bottom of the work list is denying children the chance to develop important capabilities. These include the skills of perception, hand–eye coordination and a delight in the real and imaginary worlds that they may get in no other way. The eye of the artist is different from that of the mathematician or historian, but no less important. Some teachers may argue that they have so much to do, and good artwork takes so long, that it may not get the time deserved. If that is the case we can compensate by giving our children time, materials and advice at home. We should take an interest in what pictures and

models do come home, and avoid giving our children nega-
tive messages, directly or indirectly, about the relative
importance of art compared with other kinds of work.

Music

We get to know about what children are doing in music
when they bring home a piece to practise, or the words of
the concert carols to learn. It is important to remember that
singing, humming and making a variety of sounds will have
been some of the first things our children experimented with
when they were very young. Making 'music' is essential
to all our development. There are, however, three main
stumbling blocks to music making. Music is commonly seen
as being the province of those with unique and rare talents.
Learning to play a musical instrument can be expensive and
not all of us can afford the initial and/or continuing outlay.
The pressure to take music examinations can deter children.
Try not to be put off, and encourage your children to make
and enjoy music when they can. If your child feels that music
at school is not for him then this is an issue you should raise
with their teacher. You should expect schools to provide
good musical experiences for all of the children including
singing, music, movement and drama, and the playing of at
least some percussion instruments.

TALKING TO THE TEACHER

We can, of course, go and talk to our children's classteachers to find out how they are getting on. If you want to do just that, then the accepted thing to do is to call in or ring up and ask for an appointment. You do not have to wait for a parents' evening, nor do you have to wait until you have a grievance! Teachers are happy to talk things over – talking to parents is an important part of their job. If, on the other hand, you want to go and say how pleased you are, look at Chapter 5. It also covers what to do if you are not pleased!

ASKING YOUR CHILDREN ABOUT SCHOOL

This is a problem! And it is impossible to generalise. The key is to display interest, care and concern, without pressing hard and making yourself and your children anxious or upset. Some children seem to be able to reflect on their own performance, and what is realistically their 'best' from an early age. For other children this state is not achieved in their primary years. But this is not to say that we should not ask or, more importantly, listen to what our children say about school. It is essential that we do not limit our children's responses by asking them questions in only subject terms. It is better to ask what has been done generally rather than what maths they have done. Accounts from our children will be the main way in which get to know about such things as PE and games, the science experiment that everyone is trying, the story, assembly and friendships in the play-ground. If we narrowly label what we see as a school day then our children may well come to undervalue those activities which are not in our 'approved' list. The other point to be aware of is that our children will not tell everything that goes on, and may leave out the things we see as most important. Because they do not mention it, it does not mean it does not happen!

SUMMARY

In this chapter we have set out the pattern of assessment in schools, that is the judgements of the classteachers made throughout the year (continuous assessment) and the results of national tests taken at the ages of seven and eleven (SATs), and have pointed to the kinds of things we can learn from the work our children bring home.

We should, however, not be too reliant on any of these things in working out where our own children have got to in their intellectual development. For, when you think about your own learning, the things you value most may not always be those you put down on paper. The value of learning is its power to open doors and worlds, not how much evidence there is of it in exercise books. When you get reports saying your child is working at such-and-such a Level, it is important to view it simply as a bench-mark in a life-long process. The people working on National Curriculum assessment want it to be 'formative', that is providing pointers for the future, the next steps. With this in view, the children's results are not final, but give the children themselves, and their teachers and parents, indications about where they can go on to build on what they know and can do, and where they need more help, support and encouragement.

— 4 —

HELPING OUT AT HOME AND IN SCHOOL

A GOOD START: SKILLS FOR SCHOOL READINESS

C hildren can be given information and skills, before they start school, which may make school easier for them when they get there. Some schools are lucky enough to have a nursery on the premises, or have strong links with a local playgroup. It is then possible for teachers to let parents know some of the things that will make school 'no problem' for their children. Many more of us just do our best without any clear guidance about what the first year or so at school is like, or what will be expected of our children. But with the coming of the National Curriculum we now have access to the first things that teachers will be teaching children in school, and we can work out what skills they will need to have to tackle these Level 1 activities.

In Level 1 in English, for example, children will learn to:

- 'listen attentively, and respond, to stories and poems;

- respond appropriately to simple instructions given by a teacher;

- show signs of a developing interest in reading;

- talk in simple terms about the content of stories, or information in non-fiction books;

- begin to show an understanding of the difference between drawing and writing, and between numbers and letters.'
(*English in the National Curriculum* (1989) DES and the Welsh Office.)

In Level 1 in mathematics, for example, children will learn to:

- 'count, read write and order numbers to at least 10;

- give a sensible estimate of a small number of objects (up to 10);

- copy, continue and devise repeating patterns represented by objects/apparatus or one digit numbers;

- compare and order objects without measuring, and use appropriate language;

- sort 2-D and 3-D shapes; and

- select criteria for sorting a set of objects and apply consistently.'
(*Mathematics in the National Curriculum* (1989) DES and the Welsh Office.)

In Level 1 in science, for example, children will learn to:

- 'observe familiar materials and events in their immediate environment, at first hand, using their senses.'
(*Science in the National Curriculum* (1989) DES and the Welsh Office.)

Looking at this selection you will readily be able to spot activities which can be done at home and will support children's Level 1 learning. And we have only looked at the Core subjects. There are, of course, things you can be doing which support their schoolwork in other subjects too. We have looked carefully at 'school skills' and put them under headings which are not tied to subjects, but before we turn to these, there is one vital thing to remember: *children are people*. This seems a pretty fatuous thing to say, but what we mean is that pre-school children are whole people with their own individuality, pace of development and momentum. Adults must appreciate this and help children recognise and realise the potential offered by their uniqueness. We must resist pressing them into something for which they are not yet ready, simply because we have read it somewhere, or 'Suzy down the road can do it', or the playgroup recommends it, or because it is in the National Curriculum Level 1! And we must help them to resist those pressures too. Here are some suggestions about ways in which you can support your son or daughter before they reach school age.

Personal skills

Picture the teacher of the reception class and the tasks she has to do in the first few weeks that the children are at school. For the children it is probably the biggest period of adjustment in their lives so far. It is a time when many of them will be away from their mothers for longer than ever before. All thirty or so children will need the support and encouragement of the teacher, simply to launch into their lives. Giving this kind of emotional support, while teaching the children, makes her job a hard one. If she also has to do the instrumental chores of wiping bottoms, flushing loos, and undressing and dressing children, these are onerous and time-consuming extras to her job. What are the rest of the thirty children doing while she is helping Stella in the loo?

Help children and teachers by encouraging your child to undress and dress himself with minimal help, manage both jobs on the toilet alone, and wash his hands after using the toilet and before eating.

Coordination skills

Most small children are so active that it seems silly to discuss getting them to move – indeed many of them are constantly exploring what they can do with their bodies. However, if we make sure over the pre-school years that they repeatedly get the chance to try out jumping, standing on one leg, hopping, kicking a ball, throwing a ball and having a go at catching too, this does give them a start. They also need experience of trikes, climbing frames and other apparatus. There are children who find these activities frightening at school. Experience in another setting can reduce their fears.

We can also help our youngsters with their fine coordination, by letting them mix and pour, paint and draw, make soft models and constructions, and cut and paste. Teachers can tell you of children who, for example, are unskilled with scissors at age seven or eight. It was often these same children whose mother said they could not use scissors at home because it made a mess.

Intellectual skills

There is masses of research about children's early development. We are selecting here the ideas that suit our own experience, both with our daughter and as teachers in schools. Talking to your young children helps them to learn communication skills. Listening to them when they talk helps them to be listeners too. Speaking clearly and without patronising them with 'baby talk' gives them a good vocabulary. Tell them things such as the names of the colours, and when they can say, for example, that there is a bird on the grass, you can tell them what sort of bird it is. This kind of interaction, building a little on what they know, not only gives them more vocabulary, but also helps the development of thinking. Getting them to ask for what they need, rather than anticipating it or speaking for them, develops their language.

Above all read to them. Show them that you enjoy reading for yourself, and that you enjoy doing it with them. Look at picture books together, perhaps at a special time of day, and never forgo the story at bedtime. Sing nursery rhymes, lullabies and songs together too. Children love them and they do help with memory skills. All these activities are about developing language skills. On the whole we think in words; language development means the extension of brain power.

Children love counting rhymes. Practise counting through chanting rhymes together and counting toys and books, plates and shoes, fingers and toes. Look at shapes and sizes of things. Help them to find, for example, the 'rectangles' they can see in the sitting room, and the 'circles' in the tea set. Let them look for the biggest coat or the smallest slippers in the house. Play games like, 'which toy is smaller than this one', and so on. Let them sort out the socks in the clean washing basket, and do some 'washing-up'. All these activities have to do with what we call mathematics. There is much to do that comes before and beyond sums!

HELPING YOUR SCHOOLCHILD

Being prepared: organisation skills

Good schooling is about getting study skills and learning how to learn. Being a good student is not just about wanting to learn and being hard-working, it has to do with organising yourself too. Now it is true that some children grasp things quicker than others, but good organisation and the strategies for tackling problems will help all children. Those children who do not grasp ideas quickly should still have confidence in their understanding of how to get help and how to organise their response to that help. We can assist our own children at school by looking with them at what it is they have to assemble in order to make the most of their learning time. In schools this may be called 'time on task'. Children require help to plan what they need for the day, take it to school, get themselves ready and arrive at school on time.

When they are in school their teachers will also try to give them opportunities to develop management skills. These will include getting together what they need before they start a job, putting finished work in the right place, knowing what goes in their own drawer and tidying up after one job before starting another. The teacher puts things where the children can reach them, reminds them about tidying up, and gives them time to do it and so on. We parents can try to help by suggesting that our chldren do some of these things at home. Adequate storage space is an incentive to tidy the bedroom. Our daughter shows less reluctance to hang her coat up, since we put a coat hook low enough for her to reach!

Learning skills: listening and talking

Children frequently complain that they are not listened to, or do not get a 'fair hearing'. Before there were books, or before people could read and write, we all relied entirely on what people said. When one had to listen to get *any* information about anyone or anything, people were probably better at it. Now we have books, we are literate and we have many sophisticated means of communication, including telephones, televisions and computers. But listening has not become easier. Indeed, teachers and parents complain that children do not listen either. It takes effort and practice, and we must all make time for it. It is especially important for parents to listen because we actually want our children to go on coming to us when they are troubled about anything, and they will not do so if it seems that we do not listen. Listening is an immensely important skill and one which we can all practise more. We can help our children to become good listeners through example and real opportunity.

Aside from listening to, and talking over, what troubles our children we must act, alongside teachers, as our children's first reference source. Make the time to answer questions, to look up the answers together, and to suggest ways of finding out more about the things they are studying in school. Being a good listener and talking together will help your children with National Curriculum 'speaking and listening' at school.

Learning skills: reading

Many teachers send children home with books to read. Very few give parents any information about why they are doing this, where the book fits, if at all, into the child's schoolwork or what contribution they expect of parents. The answers are these. Teachers allow books home so that children get a chance to extend learning and the enjoyment of reading outside the classroom, and so that parents can support their children's development. The book may exceed the child's present competence. It may be quite a 'hard' book or it may be one they can read easily. If it is too difficult for the child to read, then it is for parents to read aloud and talk about with the child. If it is a 'hard' book, it is for reading and listening, so you could read a little and then get your son or daughter to read the same piece to you, or you could let them read it, a little at a time, helping them when they get stuck. If it is easy, then it may be one the child has chosen so that they can read (or re-read) with total confidence, or it may have been chosen by the teacher for confidence building or consolidation. 'A little and often' seems a good rule to adopt about reading time. Ten minutes a day can be better than half an hour, and much better than a once-a-week session, no matter how long.

To make home a place for reading, it is a good idea to have all kinds of books around from the time when our children are tiny. Books are cheap presents, perhaps too cheap when compared with toys, and will last for life. Taking pleasure in reading youself is the best way to show children that they may be missing something! There is, however, no more potent way of getting children involved in reading than the story at bedtime. Even when they are fluent readers it is a great pleasure to lie there making the pictures in their heads while mum or dad reads the text, and if it is a serial there is the excitement of looking foward to the next episode. In addition, the bedtime book gives children the opportunity to talk about stories, use their imagination and practise listening. These are opportunities not to be missed.

Reading in the National Curriculum covers the skills of tackling printed words in both fiction and non-fiction texts and the skills of looking things up. There is more about getting information under 'Topics' later in the chapter. The ideas above are to help you with reading for lifelong pleasure.

Learning skills: writing

The first thing to say about writing is 'Do not make your children do it'! In most children the skills of putting ideas and facts down on paper do come behind the skills of reading. In fact, there may never be a complete 'match' between reading and writing skills. As adult readers, whatever our choice of reading, few of us can match in our own writing what we choose to read. Add to the lag between reading and writing the time that good writing takes, and there is another reason for child resistance to thank you letters and so on. We do, however, want our children to learn to write, to write well, and to write for pleasure. Home can be the place to do writing if there is somewhere to sit comfortably to do it, and the pens, pencils and paper to do it with. Materials do not have to be elaborate or expensive. Brown office envelopes and rough paper give our daughter a lot of pleasure (and writing practice too).

The development of writing comes more easily in homes where others in the family write. Why not try writing alongside your children rather than standing over them? You will actually get those letters written that you have been meaning to for so long, and your children can compare notes with you on progress. If you feel really brave why not have a stab at a poem or a piece of verse together? The refreshing way in which our children construct their stories and poems can often put our more experienced efforts to shame. What may be salutory for us is wonderful for the writing environment and the motivation of our children.

Learning skills: mathematics

This may seem to be a difficult part of the National Curriculum for parents to get involved in. That is not because the things studied in the National Curriculum are difficult, but because they may seem remote from the mathematics we learned at school. There are some indications about what mathematics is now like in Chapter 2. To help your children, support and encouragement are the best things you can give. You can also engage them in real-life problems, such as how much material you need for the new dress, or how many miles the car does to the litre. Other ways to get your children thinking mathematically include logic puzzle books, maze games, and computer games. These can be complex, and demand reading and orientation skills. For young children, snakes and ladders, beetle drive and other dice games make them think about numbers up to six. If you feel they know all about numbers up to six, you can always play with two dice and either add the numbers or take the smaller away from the larger before making your move. Additionally, games played with other people, in contrast to playing with the computer which can be switched off at any moment, do give children practice in 'gamesmanship'. This is important in the teamwork and group projects done under the National Curriculum.

Mathematics is as much a way of viewing and understanding the world as is reading. Unfortunately, mathematics suffers from a bad press. It is the case that most of us have been turned off mathematics at school and society reinforces being 'hopeless at maths' as a good thing! How often are we struck by the knowledge of literature that guests on the radio and TV have and how often do those same guests willingly admit to being no good at maths? Being mathematically 'illiterate' is actually as limiting as being unable to read. So, besides playing board games and doing what we instantly recognise as maths, we can extend our children's maths by impromptu puzzles, for example, spotting cylinders, triangles, and shapes that tesselate (i.e. shapes which fit together with no spaces between such as paving stones, chicken wire, bricks and window panes) when we are out for a walk or in the car. You do not need to be an expert to devise maths questions like 'How many telegraph poles are there to the kilometre?' and 'How long does thunder take to reach us after the lightning?'

Learning skills: science and technology

In Chapter 2 we talked about scientific method. Scientists try, by using this method, to be objective about our world. They look at things closely. They try to limit the number of things that can change (variables) and organise their results very carefully and so on. Children can develop scientific skills at home through the use of logic and maze games, through developing their powers of observation by really learning to look, for example, at the grain in wood, the beetle under the doormat and the fibres in their jumper. They can draw what they see in their room, or garden. They can observe, for example, the seasonal changes in the garden, the phases of the moon, the night sky and their own growth in height over time. They can learn to build models that move, kites that fly, go-karts and tents. They can learn to cook and do the washing, along the way learning about why cakes rise and what makes clothes clean. This all sounds rather like 'discovery' learning and it certainly is about children discovering things, and their discoveries being fresh and new to them. But at home, as in school, the discovery approach will not be possible without positive help. This means allowing things to happen, providing resources and being on hand to guide, suggest and help. If these few ideas make you feel out of your depth, then get a book about things that interest your children from the library and learn with your children. Learners, whether they are children or parents, are not expected to know everything. Our memories are simply not good enough for that.

Learning skills: topics, projects and investigations

The big difference parents can make to topic work is in showing interest, helping children collect what they need and not shutting off ways the children may have of thinking about the topic. If 'creepy crawlies' are the last thing to interest you, it does not mean that you cannot show your children the appropriate section in the children's public library, or let them become a crawly thing on the sitting room floor, or show them poems about bugs. Showing interest does not mean doing it for them, or getting involved in something you hate. It does have a lot to do with making it easy for them to get the information and help they need. Much of what our children do under the National Curriculum, at least at an early age, will be grounded in their own experience. So to help them with topics should not mean we need to spend money.

It is sometimes hard for us parents to strike a balance between interest and over-involvement and concern. And we sometimes have very little information to go on. Our children may not mention what they are investigating at school, or they may say they have got to have five envelopes and a piece of real silk for the following day! As schools become more 'open' places, it may actually be possible for

us to get to know some of the things the teacher is planning, so that we can help our children more.

When a topic really 'takes off' it can make a difference to how both children and parents respond to school. Some years ago one of us was teaching in a school where cross-curricular work and topics were highly valued both by colleagues and many, but not all, parents. One term we did a topic which helped the children to develop more concepts about shape and space, with maps as a focus. But there was a desire for a novel approach which would stimulate the children. They had 'done' co-ordinates and the local environment so the decision was to make the starting point fantastical. A new planet was created and land masses were put on this planet. A planet map was drawn collaboratively with the children. Having developed the map, groups of children adopted a part of the planet and made it their own through giving it a name, a flag, descriptions and so on. It was decided that the length of a year on the planet would correspond to a fortnight on Earth. All groups then met once a 'year' for a united nations conference. In the course of a year each group had to manage the affairs of their country including developing industries, tourism, making alliances and balancing their national books. Inflation was built in!

The topic did move on a long way from the original idea and a lot of enthusiasm and interest was generated. This extended to many parents. The first hint of this was when one parent called in and asked whether the inflation rate to be set in a couple of days' time might be rather lower than previously. Her son was anxious about the effects on his country's budget! This was not a complaint but rather a concern to support and help. That parent saw the value of the work but also experienced effects outside the intention of the teacher. Inflation was only two per cent that year! There were, in fact, many parents who started to get involved in the work. The topic was drawn to a close in school at the end of the term. The climax was a piece of drama in which one country was taken to an international court for alleged inhumanity: a very sophisticated event for ten- and eleven-year-olds. Some parents and their children continued the project well into the following year, construct-ing board games in the process. We can see from this anec-dote that:

- children, parents and teachers can share a common topic;

- communication between teachers and parents can be about learning, not just the outcomes of learning; and

- topics and projects can develop their own energy.

Learning skills: the arts: music, art and drama

It is possible that these areas of the curriculum are most under threat because of the demands of the National Curricu-lum Core subjects. They are therefore subjects in which parental support is important if children are to have experi-ence and, if they wish, become accomplished. We are not applauding an education system which does not make pro-vision for children to spend time on music, art and drama during school time, nor are we in support of parents who spend all their time chauffeuring their children to expensive extra lessons in music, dance or drama. There is a clear need for parents, through their governor representatives, to monitor the provision of time for work in the arts in school, and to support teachers' efforts to see that they are not left at the bottom of the subject list.

This said, there are important ways in which parents can help which are not stopping holes in an inadequate education system, nor providing expensive experiences for their own children. Art galleries and museums are still accessible to most of us. Local theatre companies still have seats for children's shows at affordable prices. Recorders are cheap and you can learn to play with your children. There is a range of music to listen to on the radio, so that our children can hear jazz and classical music as well as pop. And a family who sing together, even if only at Christmas or other festivals, is a family who are close and supportive. It doesn't matter whether or not you hit every note perfectly!

Learning skills: the humanities: history, geography and religious education

We believe that history is more than dates, world events and famous men and women. It is about continuity and tradition, memory and civilisation. That being the case, the place for families to start history is with themselves. When the children are in the mood, the tales from the past from grandma or mum are ones which give children a real feel for what it was like more than ten years ago.

Geography, too, can start with the family and what sort of community you live in, how the land is used, how far away the nearest city is, and what the rail and road links are like.

The treat activities we parents can give our children include trips to ruins and castles, museums and walled towns, seaside, mountains and lakes. Then history and geography are not just in books and maps.

Religious education and schooling is a problem for some parents. There is an assumption, broadly endorsed by the authorities, that Christianity should be taught in schools in England and Wales. The kind of moral and spiritual education you would like for your children is for you to decide. The headteacher of a school can give you an idea of some of the moral precepts adhered to in his or her school, for example, relating to the school rules and the manners and behaviour of the children there. However, whatever stance we adopt to organised religion, most of us do share a sense of morality and community within which we would like our children to live and grow. If we want them to become responsible and responsive adults then we need to share with them and talk about our values and the values of others. Television ensures that our children are much better informed about world events, wars, tragedies and environmental issues than any previous generation. They will need our help to develop and explain their own views and feelings.

Coordination skills

At the beginning of this chapter we talked about helping your children to explore climbing frames, ball skills and so on before they go to school. When they are at school these things are even more important for us to fit in. This is not because there will be an emphasis on these skills in school, but just the opposite. Research results tell us that most children take far too little exercise, and that it may affect their health in adult life. At school the impact of the National Curriculum is bound to change the proportions of time spent on various subjects. In an over-full day the teacher may expect to pare down the amount of time spent on PE and dance. Her rationale may be that there are other things to do which cannot be done outside school.

Trips to the park, dancing classes and five-a-side football

not only give children much needed exercise, they can also build confidence and self-assurance.

Confidence skills

One of the things we want for our children is that they achieve 'success', at least in some ways. Support and praise build confidence. Criticism, unless used sparingly and constructively, does not. It is difficult sometimes to have a feeling of empathy with our children when we are looking at what they can do. We want them to learn what their best is, at whatever age or stage of development they have reached, and then to try to do their best and be proud when they achieve it. In the end that does not involve invidious comparisons with what other children in their family or class can do, nor with some external adult standard of what is 'good'. While they are developing this for themselves, we need to offer support and encouragement, and praise. We can all remember times when we were little and we knew we had suddenly achieved something by our own efforts, and the adults around us did not even notice. Equally upsetting were the times when we made progress but did not manage something 'perfectly', and an adult ridiculed our efforts by saying we were too little, too stupid or foolhardy. Adults, on the whole, can avoid many situations in which they, themselves, are under-confident, or they can take steps to increase their confidence. Children do not often have that option. We must help them build confidence in what they can do and like doing and then work at transferring some of this confidence to activities they dislike.

HELPING IN SCHOOL

Some schools make the most of parent help and some resist it. There are two sets of issues here. Looking from the headteacher's point of view, the best interests of the children have to be safeguarded and the professional expertise of the teaching and ancillary staff must not be undermined. From the parent helper's point of view things are different. It is this set of problems that we will look at first.

Reasons for helping in school

There are a number of quite legitimate reasons for asking if you may help in school and they are these:

- you want to find out how your child is getting on in school;

- you want to find out how your child behaves in school;

- you want to find out something about how the class-teacher works;

- you want to express your support for the school as a whole;

- you want to get out of the house and meet people;

- you would like to go back to work and want to have something to do which will enhance your confidence in applying for jobs;

- you think you might like to work with children (maybe as a teacher) and you want to see what it is like; or

- you are hoping to return to teaching and want to sample classroom life again.

The first two of these reasons concern you and your own children. This kind of 'undercover operation' where you hopefully see your child at unguarded moments are never very satisfactory. Questions about progress and behaviour are better tackled as suggested in Chapter 3. Wanting to find out how the classteacher works is a difficult issue. A good start is to make sure you are well informed. Read the school prospectus (if there is one) and find out about the curriculum of the school, teaching methods and groupings. You can always raise anything that troubles you at this general level with the headteacher. It is not a good idea to rely on hearsay from other parents. You can then ask to talk to the class-teacher about her methods. She may be a bit wary of you because your enquiries imply criticism. If you then actually want to help in school, and in the process see the teaching methods in operation, go ahead.

There are a number of ways of expressing confidence in the school, and offering to support teachers and children during lesson time is just one of them. The others are raised in Chapter 5. If your reason for offering to help is about getting out yourself, then you have to ask yourself whether it really is children, and on the whole other people's that you want to meet. Teachers do not have time to talk to their helpers much during lesson time.

The last three reasons have to do with getting a job. Some headteachers see their role as catering for the needs of children exclusively, and would take a dim view of a parent who said that they wanted to help in school in order to get a job. That really is not sufficient reason for wanting to help, but it can be *one* of your reasons. If you want to work with children, or go back to work in teaching then it might be a good idea to tell the headteacher about your special interests and skills, so that your time can be used to mutual advantage.

The kinds of jobs parent helpers do

The range of possible things parent helpers do is enormous. However, teaching children is not among them. The kinds of things you may be asked to do, include:

- listening to children read;

- mixing paint, getting art materials ready and clearing away;

- playing number and word games with small groups of children;

- tidying cupboards, display areas and the library;

- covering new books and stamping them with the school stamp;

- mending damaged books;

- cooking with a small group of children;

- sewing, knitting or craftwork with a small group of children;

- coping with accidents like wet knickers and spilled paint; and

- delivering messages or collecting children from around the school.

Being good at helping in school

The best kind of parent helpers are those who are flexible, reliable, and have a sense of humour, together with a genuine interest in helping children. They also come forward and say what they are good at, and what they like doing, but they do not mind turning their hand to most things. Please do not say you can mount children's work on 15 metre display boards, or mix paint or make papier-maché models, if these things are right outside your experience. Ask to be shown the first time, and do not take on a job that you already know you are hopeless at. With a bit of training you probably would not be hopeless, but the teacher does not have the time to teach you as well as the children.

Parent experts

Baby experts If you are really good with very little children, or qualified to work with them, the biggest contribution to a school that you can make is to ask if you may run a crèche for every event during school hours or early evenings in the school year. If the headteacher agrees to your offer, then you are giving a service to all the parents of pre-school children, and to all their children in the school. If you are a schoolchild it is pretty unfair if mum cannot come to the harvest festival because you have a baby in the family. If babies are allowed, it is also unfair if you happen to be the elder brother or sister of the baby who ruins a school event by shouting and screaming. Besides, failing to consider the babies' needs by saying they may be allowed into an event of no interest to them, is a quite innappropriate stance for a primary school to take, where the needs of children are the most important consideration.

Education experts If you are a qualified teacher you are already sensitised to the feelings of teachers at school. They are doing the job and not you, and you must give them your support in getting on with it. Of course, if things are not going well for your child, then you know the correct ways to share your concerns with the classteacher. However, if you have a special area of interest in education, or have done research or writing, then offer your expertise. A parent expert who can give a talk or run a workshop for other parents is a valuable asset to any headteacher.

Expert jobs and hobbies

If you are at work in a job that can be shown to children in school, and you can arrange time off with your employer, or a visit by children from school, this is a way of supporting the school and letting children see what 'work' is like.

You may have a hobby which would be of interest to

children. It may, for example, be ornithology, astronomy or fishing. Or you may be a collector of, say, postcards, gloves or bicycles. Whatever your interest, if you can share it with children, ask the headteacher if you may. The enthusiasm, interest and study skills used on hobbies are the same as those children and teachers need to cultivate in school!

SUMMARY

For our children school is a part of their lives. For us it is easy to see school and home as separate, and school as different from family life. But schooling and home life, weekends and holidays are all a continuity for children. It is the way life is! On these grounds alone it is important that we support our children in their whole lives and we can do so by taking an interest in their learning and also by being active in aspects of their learning. Not all things can or should be learned at school. Some learning needs to be undertaken in the home. In this chapter we have indicated a variety of ways in which we can support our children. These include pre-school activities, listening and sharing, and the extension of our children's experiences. We also see that, for some parents, there is the possiblity of going into school and supporting opportunities for teachers and children.

— 5 —

PRAISING AND
COMPLAINING

Those of us whose children are already in primary school are continually thinking about, if not talking about, what our children's school experiences are like. We often comment on the effects of these experiences on ourselves and the rest of the family. We write on reading cards, 'Maxine did enjoy her reading book and we laughed aloud at the bit where . . .' We tell the neighbour, 'Brian is happier about going to school now that the teacher has given him a special job to do.' We say to parents we know, that the new teacher is very good and the projects she does are really interesting, that our son's reading has suddenly improved this term and that the Christmas concert was lovely.

On the other hand we also complain about, for example, the state of our children's clothes after a schoolday, the bullying at playtime, the reading books that are too difficult or too easy and the classrooms that look drab and uninviting. Many of these kinds of remarks are made to people other than teachers, who could do something about them.

This chapter is about making our compliments reach the people they should, and how, when necessary, to complain to good effect.

GIVING PRAISE

When you are pleased say so! Children, parents and teachers do not get enough praise. When were you last praised by the boss, your partner, your parents, your friends or your children? Even if it was a long time ago, you can probably still recall how good it made you feel. Praise not only makes us feel good, it also makes us more confident.

To praise more we have to abandon the 'British' stance of reticence and cool appraisal in favour of mutual support. Education is about personal growth and we can contribute genuinely to this by giving open recognition of things done well. This means praising parents, children and teachers alike for we are all involved in the educative process.

Praising children

Praising children does not mean we have to praise everything that they do regardless of effort, achievement or expectation. We should praise them, however, every time they do something which indicates personal growth. Praise is, in our view, essential to such growth. There are so many opportunities for children to demonstrate growth in the early years of schooling, that there is no shortage of occasions for praise.

For example, we expect them to go into school independently, to look after their belongings, to be outgoing with other children and with adults, and to do as they are told. They may not have had to do all these things all the time when at home with mum. At home it is things like kissing uncle, managing the toilet alone, getting dressed without help or 'eating up' which deserve praise. Once our children are settled in school we are often inclined to concentrate mainly on academic achievement. Praise for good work and examination success is great but there are other things which are often much more important such as:

- saying how they feel about something that happened in the playground;

- joining in willingly, and helping others;

- producing what they know to be their 'best work', not just what is seen as good by adults; and

- letting another child have first go, and sharing things.

The list of achievements is different for each of our children. The steps our children make need regular and appropriate praise to help nurture their positive and continued development towards confidence and self-determination in adulthood. They, in their turn, can then give praise.

Praising teachers

There is nothing more encouraging to a teacher than to have a parent come along and say how pleased they are with what is happening in school. There are incidents that stand out in our own teaching careers which still give us pleasure. There was the occasion when a mother came to a parents' evening and gave the teacher a hug to say 'thanks for everything'. There was the time when a father who seemed to fit the doorway in both directions, stamped into the room and reached inside his mac only to pull out two bottles of brown ale. He banged them down on the desk and said, 'My son's doing all right with you', and walked out!

All too often teachers hear nothing but complaints and the pleased parents stay away. There can be a number of reasons for this. Teachers are authority figures and our own memories of school may make teachers seem aloof. We may sense that we might be seen to be patronising, or we may feel tongue-tied and under-confident about our ability to express our feelings in a balanced way. However, it is worth remembering that the teacher you wish to praise will certainly be understanding and empathic, so say it anyway. They will get great pleasure from your message, and the praise may, incidentally, help their confidence too. Such growth is not just the prerogative of children.

When you begin to feel positively involved in your children's schoolwork, let the teacher know by saying so. Here are some examples:

'Duncan is so excited about the new project. Is there something we can do to help at home?'
or
'Patty enjoyed the maths quiz so much, may she have another copy to test out on us?'
or
'Can you tell us where we can find out more about telecommunications, or logic or tessellation.'

When teachers are assured by our remarks, that they have our trust and support, they feel more confident about their ability to work with and for our children.

Adding to the school's reputation

If you continue to feel very positive about your children's teachers tell other people too. By telling the headteacher, your praise may enhance the teacher's reputation in the eyes of the head, and since it is he or she who will provide a reference for the classteacher's next job, you may thereby enhance the teacher's career prospects. It is tempting to hold back on giving praise if you feel that this may actually help the teacher to leave, but teachers need new challenges in order to retain their zest and commitment.

You can also tell other parents, but do not be surprised if they do not share your feelings. A teacher who does wonders for one child may not do the same for another. Teaching 'style' is an important factor in how children respond to their schoolwork. However, National Curriculum delivery is dependent on teachers presenting ideas and opportunities in a number of ways. One aspect of a school's reputation rests on what the parents think of it, so by praising its teachers you are adding to its reputation.

Actions as well as words There are ways of expressing your support for the school, other than by just saying so. You could consider doing some of the following to support what you say:

- You can offer your time to assist the school, either by helping on the PTA committee if there is one, or by going into school during school time (as in Chapter 4), or by standing for election as a parent governor.

- You can offer financial help to the school by joining in a lottery or covenant scheme. This is an issue for your own conscience. Parents should not be asked, and headteachers should not be forced to ask for help in providing the basic necessities for the school. That said, the money given by parents should go, without strings, to the school to buy what is needed. Too many parents want to be credited with contributing to some 'high profile' luxury that can be reported on in the local press and wheeled out for visitors. If the school needs a carpet, or library books, let the money be spent on that.

- You can support the school in competitions and sports activities. It is important to be sensitive to the idea that competition needs leavening with cooperation, and vice versa. Too often one is emphasised at the expense of the other. For example, in playing team games, it is clear that to score more points or goals than the opposing team is only possible through cooperative activity. We need to extend children's ability to cooperate. It is vital that we help our children, indeed all children, to value all contributions to a common effort and not exclude cooperation through competition. The appropriate future use of world resources depends on collaborative effort. Whilst this may seem remote from the school playing field, it is the case that we all need to see ourselves in a group setting and, in supporting team games, we can nurture the ability to collaborate. It really is true that taking part is more important than winning!

Praise and the National Curriculum

In this book we are trying to support you in engaging, with your children, in positive involvement in the National Curriculum. It follows, therefore, that there are aspects of National Curriculum work which we should be careful to praise. It is not just a case of looking at what children now know. We should also give particular emphasis to:

Progression Where is Samantha now compared with a few months ago? What has she achieved in terms of her confidence? What new insights does she have?

Connections What areas of experience is Sheena now bringing together?

Study skills How is Stuart organising himself for work, compared with a year ago?

Outlook   How is Jafet now viewing his own learning and how does he approach new tasks?

Cultural   This includes aesthetic, religious and moral development. So how does Myra feel about her own community and the whole of society? What concerns her? Does William feel he can help enhance the quality of life in his village? What issues is William getting to grips with now?

Academic   Finally . . . How is Rory appraising his own work, and developing an idea of what is his best? What are his ways of reacting to test situations and results, compared with a while ago?

Praising yourself

In praising our children and the teachers who give them learning and social opportunities we can be forgiven, occasionally, for feeling left out and under-valued. Who comes around and says what a great mother or father you are? There are support groups, particularly for mothers, but on the whole the help they offer is instrumental, and relieves the burdens of parenting. There is not much personal praise handed out. Perhaps we could start with our husbands, wives and partners. It may seem laughable to say things like, 'After all these weeks of problems at bedtime, you did a great job of getting the kids to sleep tonight!' but it does let us know that we don't take each other for granted *all* the time!

MAKING A COMPLAINT

If you want to complain about an aspect of the school there are a number of things you can do. There is, however, an accepted order in which to do them. If you follow the order, first you cannot be accused of being high-handed, and second you may get things sorted out before people in authority outside the school are drawn in. Before we look at the

order to follow when making a complaint, there are two preliminary points to think about.

Thinking it through Before talking to anyone official, sort out exactly what it is that you want to complain about. Discuss it, in confidence with someone in the family, or with a friend. The section at the end of this chapter on 'Causes for comment' will help to unravel some of the major issues. Also, try to reflect on what you can reasonably hope to achieve in terms of outcome. When *you* know where you are starting from, and that your expectations are realistic, you can start complaining! Act before things have built up and seriously affect you and your child.

Firmness and assertiveness in women In our society it can be difficult for women to approach people in authority and make a strong case without getting the reputation for being tearful, hysterical or illogical. This is patently pernicious nonsense. However, because women are said to have that aura, if you are a woman with a complaint, make the most of your chances. Go in to school promptly for a pre-arranged appointment, looking tidy and with a calm and temperate air!

TO WHOM TO COMPLAIN

Start by making an appointment to see the teacher or teachers involved. From there, if all is not sorted out, ask for an appointment to see the headteacher. If you still feel aggrieved contact one of the governors and ask to talk to them.

Of course, there are people who can be approached at the local education authority offices. Education authority officials will, on the whole, start by taking a defensive stance towards their schools. It weakens your position if you go there before doing all you can to resolve the problem at school level.

Talking to the classteacher

- Be prepared to speak *and* listen.

- Try not to be so extreme that there is no room for compromise either on your own part or on the teacher's.

- State your case clearly and carefully, without shouting and using immoderate language; you will be heard out more sympathetically if you are civilised.

- When you feel you have made your point and you have heard the teacher out, try for some action by asking, 'What do you think we can do now?' or 'What are we going to try?' This actually gives the teacher the opportunity to suggest some kind of team effort. Even if you feel your views are diametrically opposed to the teacher's, the fact is that the problem does have to be sorted out by both of you.

- If you still feel that nothing will happen as a result of your meeting, say so; and then you can suggest another strategy that may be attempted, but try to compromise a little if necessary.

- Finally suggest another meeting; then you can both say

whether things have improved, and because you have already requested the discussion, neither of you will feel in confrontation.

Talking to the headteacher

If you try all this with the classteacher and the problem still remains unresolved, then ask if you may have an appointment with the headteacher. Employ the same approach as we suggested above, but do appreciate that no headteacher will undermine or be critical of one of the teachers whilst talking to you. If the head sees your point and decides to take action then you must expect this to happen subsequent to your meeting. The best you are likely to achieve at the meeting with the head is a commitment to look into the matter further. Some time must, therefore, be allowed for the head to bring about change. Assuming that the head does cause the teacher to change some aspect of her approach, it is vital that you do not further undermine that teacher's position by broadcasting what you believe to be the effect of your intervention. Good working relationships need fostering and should not be prejudiced by the glorification of short-term 'victories'.

Talking to others

Should you still feel extremely dissatisfied with the effects of your complaint, you are entitled to discuss the issue with a school governor. Commonly, your first approach will be to a parent governor. What governors will normally do is to listen and ask questions, in order to be absolutely certain of the nature of your complaint. They will then raise the matter with the headteacher. This need not wait for a governors' meeting; heads would normally expect to see governors regularly for feedback purposes and to keep governors in touch with what is happening at school. If a governor makes promises beyond raising the matter then be suspicious. Whilst it is true that governors do have a lot of responsibilities and authority, this is collective and a majority of governors would be needed to carry through, say, the changing of school procedures and rules.

Finally, you do have the possibiliy of talking to people in the local education authority office. Do not be daunted by bureaucracy, you can and will be able to talk to an officer there. These officers can put your complaint into context, for they know of the practices within a number of schools in the locality. They will also tell you whether they see your complaint as reasonable and will help with the feasibility or desirability of particular courses of action. It is only on rare occasions that problems cannot be cleared up at the school level, but if this is the case, it must be discussed with local authority personnel so that matters can be finally resolved.

MOVING SCHOOLS

If after all this you decide that the best thing for your child would be to move him to another school, then this is your prerogative. However, you do need to check the following:

- Will the new school be different from the one you know? You do not want to leap from a situation where the issues have, at least, been aired, to one where you have to start again on the same problems.

- Have you been honest about the problem, to youself, your child and the teachers? A record of 'the story so far' will go to the new school, so it is not quite the fresh start you may hope for.

- Will the gains made by your family, through changing schools, outweigh the loss of friends, routines and much that is familiar in your child's daily life?

THE EFFECTS OF A COMPLAINT

Making a complaint will affect three sets of people and all the relationships between them. It will affect you (the parents), the teachers to whom you speak (and maybe other teachers in the school if the issue is shared in confidence), and all your children, not just the one concerned in the complaint.

For yourself, you should try to be optimistic about the outcome and not feel undermined by anything challenging the teachers may say. The teachers, whatever their personal reactions, will expect civility from you, just as you do from them. You certainly need to be courteous, for you may need to talk again at a future date. Your child who is at the centre of the problem, needs support to carry on as usual. It is not wise to assume that he or she will be unaffected by your complaining, but nor should you assume that they will be victimised.

Always keep in mind that there are two main objectives in making a complaint: first you want a change in the situation, and second you want life to be 'normal' afterwards. With these things in mind it is important to follow the procedures properly and to avoid putting anyone, yourself included, into a position from which the only escape is dramatic. Confrontation will not meet the needs of the situation, but clarity of argument and certainty of approach will enhance the possibilities of a fruitful outcome for everyone concerned.

You will find that some of the issues in schooling that make you want to complain may be just the aspects that other parents feel very positive about! For this reason we shall now discuss examples of a range of typical causes for compliment and/or complaint.

CAUSE FOR CONCERN

Fairness

We have put this first because we think it may be at the root of many complaints. Adults and children tend to put fairness at the top of the list of things they expect a teacher to be. It simply does not seem fair if your child is never chosen for anything, does not get his pictures on the wall, or is sent out of assembly for being naughty more often than the other children. Now, it may be that the teacher behaved quite appropriately in all these situations. However, what is not fair is that your child does not appear to be getting support and encouragement for things that do go well. At least you are not getting to hear about it.

Work not being done in school

You really have a cast iron case here if the requirements of the National Curriculum are not being met. You can find out what these are by asking to see the documents in school, or by acquiring a copy from your local library.

If your comments are about work not done which cannot be seen as part of the National Curriculum, you will have to be extremely persuasive indeed, and have the real (not just notional) support of other parents to get the teachers to change. They may resist the insertion of any more work into the school's curriculum because they are already person-ally hard-pressed. There are many potent arguments made by teachers about their use of time, and there may not be enough school time to do more than the nationally set requirements. But you must be certain that school time is actually being well spent before you accept that certain things are not offered. Parents should not be deterred in trying to ensure a balanced curriculum. It is vital that we parents do not let the arts and physical education, for example, fall out

of the timetable because the National Curriculum demands in other subjects are unrealistic.

Teaching methods

To some extent these will always be idiosyncratic. Every teacher is different and it is within their professional brief to implement the teaching methods which suit them and the children in their care. However, they are also required to meet the needs of each and every individual child. If your child does not thrive on certain aspects of the methods used, then it is quite appropriate to discuss with the teacher how your child may be better helped at school through, for example, more supervision, more independence, more individual projects or even things like using his own crayons.

Assessment

The National Curriculum carries with it an elaborate system of assessment, but it will be some years before teachers are familiar with all they have to do. The system is rigorous and uses external tests. Added to these are the teacher's own judgements which are still likely to be the most potent indicator of performance. While in the past teachers have often been expected to be exclusively judges of *present* performance, National Curriculum assessment also carries the idea of identifying *potential*. This is of very great importance to children and to us, their parents. It is much more important that parents and children know something about future capability than past achievement. We may now see a shift in teachers' skills towards potential, through their use of National Curriculum assessment.

Performance results are already in the past, so do not waste time and goodwill by complaining that 'Johnny did not get a high enough mark for his essay.' What you can and should complain about, when necessary, is if reports and assessments made by the teacher give no indication of what Johnny should be doing next, that is, the reports should tell you what strengths and skills he can build on, and what aspects need more work.

Relationship with teacher

Teachers should be able to create good 'business' relationships with all the children in their care. Children should be able to make similarly 'good' relationships, and they need our help to do so. Our school system rests on a principle of the collective, that is the group, class or school. Children are required to stick by the collective rules, or they are labelled 'bad' or 'strange'. It does not compromise their individuality if they stick by the rules, so we must assure our own children that they can work the system best by acknowledging the rules which govern that particular ocmmunity. If there are excessive restrictions then you are better placed than your children to challenge silly rules and petty regulations.

The National Curriculum requirements do make it clear that it is individual effort and progress that needs constant monitoring. We may see a welcome shift in teachers' focus away from the whole class to individuals and small groups within it. Not only will this be necessary for successful National Curriculum implementation, it is also desirable because it increases the possibilities of closer relationships between teacher and individual children. Teachers may then come to accommodate more readily individual differences and creative effort in response to work set.

Bullying and loneliness

In our view, schools are often the worst places in which to make and keep friends. This may be because some aspects of school life are unlike the 'real' world. For example, no-one, outside a school that is, would ask 200 or more children to play peaceably in a confined but barren space. If you have ever been to the first day of the sales, or in a crowded swimming pool in a heatwave, or in the tube in rush hour, you may recall that you do not feel very friendly in these kinds of situations either. Nor would we ask children to line up in single file, then make them wait for twenty minutes, and expect them to remain civil to one another at the end of it. If you, as an adult, have to wait twenty minutes for a bus, it can be demanding on your patience. If you do so at the end of a queue of thirty people, you feel even worse.

However, a school plan which abandons playtimes and lunch queues is probably not a likely outcome of the National Curriculum, so the best we can do is arm ourselves, and our children, with ways of coping with the minuses of school life. Our children may be the bullies or the bullied, the lonely or the afraid. Our first approach must be to try to make things easier with our own children, and below is a list of things which may help. You will need to assess which seem most appropriate to you, as some are rather unorthodox. If a child seems unhappy, we must do everything in our power to reduce that child's unhappiness. If a problem occurs only in class time, take it up with the classteacher, but if it happens at playtime or any other time of day, discuss it with both the classteacher and the headteacher.

Bullies and the bullied It is tempting to think of these children as different from our own. This is absolutely untrue. The problem is one for all of us and all our children. Recent research shows shamefully high levels of bullying in Britain's schools, with something like one in five children suffering. Bullies and the bullied are not born so; they become so. As we have said, it may be in part due to the privations of many playgrounds. The rest of the explanation, in our view, rests with all of us. There needs to be a shift away from individual success at any price, to a more compassionate idea of how we treat one another. For schools, the immediate problems are those of playground and playtime organisation, appropriate and real supervision, and the status and role of dinner ladies.

We parents need to ensure our children understand these things:

- **Always** respond by getting adult help when a fight is threatened.

- **Always** tell on a bully even if it is not you he is bullying.

- **Always** tell the truth.

- Words can be just as hurtful as blows, so try not to hurt people with either.

The lonely and fearful Here are some positive things to try, that may relieve loneliness and fear:

- Invite a classmate home to tea.

- Invite a classmate and their mum to have a cup of tea straight after school.

- Give your child a comfort toy for their pocket at playtime.

- Give them a snack they can share.

- Give them a pocket-sized joke book.

- Give them a hand puppet to play with at playtime (the puppet may be more confident in conversation than its owner).

- Advise them to hold the hand of the teacher.

- Advise them to hold their best friend's hand.

- Give them a mascot to sit in their pocket or on the desk.

- Give them a talisman, like a large coat button, which they can rub and become 'brave'.

These are only piecemeal measures in what needs to be a concerted effort to help all children to feel more secure, confident and humane.

SUMMARY

In this chapter we have stressed the need to see praise as being centrally important for all of us, whether children or adults, teacher or parent. We see praise as being the essential fuel for the drive to personal esteem and self-worth. An essential purpose of any educational system must be to support individuals in developing self-determination. It is important to realise that realistic self-appraisal, and congratulation, needs the climate of group and other individuals' approval. We cannot become balanced individuals with a healthy, but questioning respect for others and the world in which we live, without the experience of praise from others. We continue to need praise for things really well done. In this respect we must emphasise that praise must not be gratuitous – it must relate to the appropriate area of personal growth. These areas may be different for each of us.

We have also discussed the kinds of issues you may raise with teachers and how to complain. If you have a real grievance, do not hold back from raising it. We have to champion the children's cause in education – sometimes there is no-one else who will.

— 6 —

CHILDREN'S NEEDS AND PARENTS' RESPONSIBILITIES

YOUR CHILD'S EXPERIENCE

A child's view of the world If we reflect on our own schooldays, there are incidents we can recall vividly as being very important which, now that we are adult, seem inconsequential. We have accrued so much experience since then that it is sometimes difficult to view the world as a child. To understand our own children's school experience it is important, though, that we try to see the world from their point of view. Getting told off, doing something that is not allowed, being found out or wrongly accused can be torture to a six-year-old and we need to be able to say, with conviction, 'I know just how you feel'.

To be an understanding parent means three things. The first is that we know that children may view the world differently from us but accept that their view is just as valid. The second is to champion children in the face of other adults; and finally we must always be on the side of right. This sounds like a job description for a super hero. We have to try it without unique powers or magic words!

School and home For children, the number and quality of the links between school and home will depend mainly on how home and school compare as experiences. For some

young children it may be that school is not somewhere 'different', an institution apart from home with a separateness about it, but is part of a continuous experience. This may explain why some small children assume their teacher sleeps under the desk in the classroom! For other children, a grasp of the school as a temporary community of people who meet together and then go away to lead home lives, comes when they are very small. The biggest difference in perspective between our view, as parents on the outside, and children themselves comes from the fact that for children home and school are compulsory!

BOYS VERSUS GIRLS

All of the things we discuss in this book apply equally to men and women teachers. Additionally, whether the teacher is a man or woman will itself affect the way the children behave and possibly affect their learning.

Everyone is influenced by their upbringing and the expectations placed on them. These expectations are different for boys than girls. We, as parents, do have the capacity to modify these expectations and we should exercise this option and use our influence. However, in furthering the rights of all of our children to be treated equally in terms of the opportunities offered to them, it is necessary to know if there are predetermined differences between boys and girls and, importantly, the effects these have on how they are treated in school.

Apparent differences in learning skills

There is much research to suggest that there are learning differences between the sexes. For example, girls seem to excel in language skills while boys are better at mathematics and reasoning. Boys seem to do better in some kinds of tasks than girls. This is noted by the Task Group on Assessment and Testing, set up by the Government as an advisory group. In their report (HMSO 1988) they say, for example, in tests 'The multiple choice format appears to favour boys as does practical testing.' (V para 24.)

Whilst there is much discussion of the similarities and possible differences between boys and girls, evidence on these things is inconclusive. Our experience as teachers, and as parents, makes us believe that the environment in which children grow up is very important in determining how they will view themselves, their friends of both sexes and their ability to grasp learning opportunities. Differences indicated by research on samples of boys and girls do not mean that no boys are good at English and that all girls are hopeless at maths!

Differences in learning opportunities

It is even more important that we understand that despite the differences in learning we have mentioned, girls in general are doing better than boys, across all subjects, at the top of the primary school. By the time girls reach the age of thirteen or fourteen, there is a dramatic reversal of this trend, and boys out-perform girls consistently after that. This is disturbing information for parents of girls, but parents of boys should be equally concerned about the provision of equal opportunities. In order for society to progress in a balanced way we must have an educational system which offers equal opportunities for both boys and girls. It is no more fun for boys to be labelled as active providers than it is for girls to be labelled as passive dependents! To counter the dangerous effects of stereotyping, we parents should make sure that our children, both boys and girls, have access in school to a broad range of themes and concepts and are allowed to tackle these in a variety of ways. For example, girls and boys should have the chance to:

- learn poetry, write it and act it out dramatically themselves and with puppets;

- do experiments which involve collecting information and tabulating results, and drawing conclusions;

- try to find a variety of solutions to practical problems, such as the quickest route to the newsagent, or the cheapest sources of protein for a family meal, or how to plant up the vegetable plot for the best yield;

- use calculators, computers, tape-recorders and videos with confidence and competence;

- skip and dance and play ball games;

- draw, make models, sing and make music;

- find out from books, films, visits and by talking to people, about times past and other parts of the world; and

- take delight in mathematical patterns and puzzles.

Fortunately, the National Curriculum makes all this mandatory for teachers. It is difficult to imagine how they could hope to cover its requirements without using a variety of

methods and tasks. Good teaching of the National Curriculum should not prove advantageous to one sex rather than the other. Rather it should enable both boys and girls to engage with a broad (or in some schools, broader) range of human experience.

Sex-stereotyping by parents and teachers

Beyond the possible sex-linked differences in tackling thinking and learning there are far more insidious ways in which one sex may get the advantage over the other. And as far as learning is concerned it is more often boys who get the better deal than girls. The perpetrators of this unfairness are parents and teachers alike.

A common argument raised in favour of giving the sexes different opportunities is that girls and boys are *not* the same, and that they force the difference by announcing their preferences. Differences there undoubtedly are, but they may not be as great as we suppose, for there are subtle pressures on children, from birth, to conform to a gender-linked image. Most adults conspire in this by, for example, allowing a different range of behaviours from boys than girls, and

expecting a different rate of intellectual growth and performance from each.

We also tend to reinforce stereotypes in our choice of toys.
Toy manufacturers exploit these stereotypes and parents go
along with them. Construction toys are commonly seen as
being appropriate as boys' presents. These toys promote an
understanding of spatial concepts, and they have to be made
available and attractive to both boys and girls, at home and
at school, for all children to have spatial concept opportunity.
A dolls' house is often seen as a 'role-play' toy where, typically, little girls can act out stereotyped roles in the home
and talk a lot while they play. Like construction toys, this
kind of toy has to be equally available to both sexes for equal
opportunity.

We recall, as teachers, that we had to deliberately set out
to avoid prejudice in setting work for children, and allowing
them equal (and sometimes even 'special') access. For example, despite there being a range of toys available to all the
children in the class, there was the little boy who really
wanted to play with the dolls' house but never chose to. At
the end of the day he often volunteered to 'tidy it up',
because he could do so without affecting his image. There
are girls who avoided lego, but with active encouragement
and a stimulus like 'make a hamster cage, a proscenium arch,
a garden centre or a dragon' made models as enthusiastically
and successfully as boys.

We parents really have to check signs of sexism in school
and remark on the following things:

- Does the teacher allocate tasks on the basis of sex. For
  example, do girls always do washing up? Do boys usually
  make models and produce diagrams for displays while the
  girls do the writing?

- Are work groups divided into 'all boys' and 'all girls' and
  is there a legitimate reason for this?

- Does the teacher actively discourage stereotyping by the children themselves?

- Does the teacher avoid making sexist remarks, such as 'boys will be boys' or 'boys don't cry' or 'don't try those feminine wiles on me'?

- Does the teacher spend more time with or give more attention to boys than girls?

- Does the teacher praise girls and boys for different things? For example, are girls praised for neat work, and boys for ingenious solutions to problems?

- Are girls given as much help and the same kind of help when they get stuck with their learning?

- Does the class and school library have plenty of non-sexist books?

It is worth reiterating that sexism applies to boys as well as girls. Much of what we have said indicates that, in school, girls seem to get a worse deal than boys. However, in our experience, boys are continually pressured into the strong competitive forceful male mould as much at school as anywhere else. Part of this pressure comes from the same teachers who have firm ideas about what girls should be like.

The National Curriculum documents do not set down specific things which teachers should to do avoid stereotyping, but they do make it clear that all children should have access to everything in the curriculum. Principles of equal access for all and the necessity of meeting individual needs carry underlying assumptions that teachers will be unbiased and even-handed to both sexes.

SEX EDUCATION IN PRIMARY SCHOOLS

Before the introduction of a National Curriculum it was not compulsory for schools to provide sex education. In schools where we have worked, it was raised at lower junior level (at age seven to nine), and parents were always consulted for their permission before the lessons were given, and they were able to withdraw their children by keeping them at home on the appropriate days.

In the National Curriculum provisions for science, Attainment Target 3 at Level 4 states that children should learn about reproduction in mammals. Work at this Level will probably be done at upper junior level (at age nine to eleven). It is compulsory, and parents are not given the option of removing their children from such lessons.

School governors, in consultation with the headteacher and the local education authority can determine the amount and tenor of sex education within a school. The school's policy about sex education should then be made available to parents, in a written brochure or school handbook. Many parents like sex education to be carried out in school. It is through our parent governors that we parents can try to ensure that the subject is treated sensitively and appropriately.

However, there are moral, social, mental and physical aspects to sex education to consider, and we think the prime place to raise all these issues is at home, and the best people to teach them are mum and/or dad. We do not mean giving a one-off lecture to your child when you think they are ready, but answering questions as they arise, making sure they have all the facts and understand about the moral and emotional dimensions before adolescence.

There are some parents who are concerned that sex information leads to premature sexual activity. The statements of health education experts indicate that the reverse is the case;

that is that sound accurate information is a guard against such activity.

RELIGIOUS EDUCATION AND EXPECTATIONS OF SCHOOLS

Headteachers are required to ensure that religious education is carried out in their schools, in accordance with the 1944 Education Act. Alongside the development of the National Curriculum documents there have been Government statements to say that this should broadly adhere to Christian beliefs and follow a locally agreed syllabus. Syllabuses compiled in the future must take account of other major faiths.

There must also be assemblies, but it is up to the head and governing body of the school to decide whether these should always involve the whole school, or whether a class or group of classes can convene their own assembly.

Parents may withdraw their children from assemblies if they wish, though there is no rule to say that the school must keep children busy at these times. Children may also be withdrawn from religious education lessons, and if you feel worried about religious education going on in your child's school, go and discuss the matter with the head-teacher, to sort out the specific areas of concern. Remember, the children are being taught *about* Christianity.

If you have strong views about the necessary religious education of your children, it is best, ideally, to find out what happens in a school before sending them there. Historically, schools were heavily dependent on the Church. Voluntary Controlled schools are those where the Church owns the buildings but now has minimal financial involvement. A minority of the governing body are from the Church and the local education authority are the employers of the staff. In Controlled schools the religious education syllabus follows that recommended by the local authority. However, if sufficient parents of children at a Controlled school make representation, the school can adopt the syllabus provided by the diocesan board of education.

By contrast, Voluntary Aided schools are those where the Church not only owns the buildings, but has full financial obligations regarding them. For these schools the majority of the governors are from the church, and the governors are directly responsible for staff employment policies. For Aided schools, advertisements for new teachers will often say that a communicant or practising member of the Church of England, or Roman Catholic Church or a commited Christian is preferred, and the parish priest will be a member of the school governing body and will be influential in the selection of new staff. The religious education syllabus operating in these schools is determined by the diocese. In both Controlled and Aided schools you can expect the parish priest to come in regularly to give assemblies and talk to the children, and for the children to visit the local church. The amount of contact the children have with the Church will vary from school to school, but may be greater in Aided schools.

County primary schools are managed by the local authority without strong church links. It is the headteacher and governors who determine the extent of the religious time-table in these schools, in accordance with local education authority policy.

MULTICULTURAL QUESTIONS: ORIGINS AND UPBRINGING

The National Curriculum is to be made available for every child in a State school in England and Wales. It seems that the intention has been to provide for the indigenous population without taking into account special cultural requirements or the needs of members of minority groups. The aim has not been to offend, nor has anything been written into the National Curriculum with the intention of alienating people of different races or religions, but the absence of any real consideration of culture and the curriculum may cause diffi-culties for some parents.

One of the real dangers in producing a National Curricu-lum, whatever country is producing it, is the imposition of a fixed mono-cultural view of knowledge. This applies to all aspects of all subjects. To spell out the links between English and Welsh society and each strand of thought in the National Curriculum would take more space than this book allows. You can reflect on the British western democratic bias in what is taught in our schools in, for example, English (of course!) mathematics, science, art, music, and so on.

It is no surprise to us that one of the most contentious areas under discussion in the National Curriculum is history. History is a subject which, along with religious education, is a major vehicle for informing children of their cultural roots and of cultural change and development. History teaches us that the people of England and Wales are what they are today through the exchange and interplay of differ-ent cultures. For the continued healthy development of all nations we must ensure that cultural exchange and understanding, along with the richness of cultural difference, is supported and not inhibited in schools. This can be done by allowing all children to find out about the community in which they now live, and their own origins and the lives of those communities in times past. Understanding can also be achieved through helping children to see themselves as having individual rights and responsibilities in the community they live in, to work with everyone for everyone. It is up to teachers and parents to work together to help this understanding.

With our support, all children can be helped to self-determining adulthood, when they can compare and contrast human ideas without prejudice about where the ideas came from, and can contribute through the way they, themselves live, to a world where people do not exploit one another in any way.

In the booklet offering information to teachers about the National Curriculum, (*National Curriculum: From Policy to Practice*, DES, 1989), there are hints that the compilers of the National Curriculum documents have not overlooked multicultural issues entirely. The booklet reminds teachers that the whole curriculum includes, for example, personal and social education, coverage of gender and multicultural issues, and political and international understanding.

If there are National Curriculum requirements which deeply offend your beliefs and practices, you should first of all talk to the teaching staff in your children's school – they may be able to offer practical help and advice. If you follow the procedure we suggested in Chapter 5, on making a complaint, you will get to talk to the right people. If you feel strongly enough, and your views are shared by other parents, you may consider organising a group to represent your views to the school and local authority. But remember, teachers, no matter how sympathetic they are to your cause, do have to conform to the law.

SPECIAL NEEDS

It has always seemed a bit strange to us that some children should be declared to have 'special needs' in law. Every child has needs, and for each individual they are special. What is meant is that there are children for whom the universally offered facilities in schools are inappropriate or insufficient. In the National Curriculum Council's booklet entitled, *A Curriculum for All: Special Educational Needs in the National Curriculum* (1989), it says that these children include a range of young people from those with '. . . profound and multiple disabilities which are experienced by a minority of pupils and call for life-long support to the sometimes less apparent educational problems of those who, for example, have intermittent hearing loss.' (p. 1).

It is important to note that 'all pupils share the right to a broad and balanced curriculum, including the National Curriculum.' However, '. . . the right to share in the curriculum . . . does not automatically ensure access to it, nor progress within it.' (ibid. p. 1).

If your child is labelled as having special needs, it is the duty of the school to provide maximum access to the National Curriculum and enable optimum progress for him or her, when his or her difficulties have been taken into account. An official 'Statement' will be completed if or when it has been established that a child needs additional resources. Some children's difficulties are such that they are seen to have special needs at school from the outset. If this is the case with your child, you can choose a school with his or her specific needs in mind. Whether your child's needs are discovered sooner or later, you do need to become an expert on a number of things. They include: finding out exactly what your child's difficulties are and asking about what effect the difficulties will have on his or her education; and getting to know how your child feels about the opportunities and facilities provided in school, and keeping in constant touch with the teachers about how you and your child feel.

When you think you have ensured that your child is in the best school for his or her needs, it is then important that you have the extra support from teachers in being realistic about your child's educational difficulties and any resulting limitations, so that you can help at home in giving confidence without frustration.

If your child is exempt, even temporarily, from some part of the National Curriculum, you should have been consulted and you do have a right of appeal if you are not in agreement about the exemptions. You can find out more about this from the school's headteacher.

From what we have said, we can see that some official views of children with special educational needs are that they are children with disabilities or medical problems which range from very severe to only slight. However, teachers use a broader definition of special needs, to include those children with no apparent physical problem, whose attainment is well below what the teacher sees as 'average' for the age group she teaches. We have called these children low attainers, and by this we mean to indicate children whose learning achievements fall below those that might be expected for a child of their age. The National Curriculum Levels within Attainment Targets will be used, by teachers, to identify low attainers. Low attainment may be a product of behaviour as much as intellectual capability.

In addition to the identification of low attainment there has been, over recent years, a move to identify special needs in relation to 'gifted' children. These children are seen as those who have particular talents and who are capable of high attainment in one or more curriculum area. The concern for these children is that they may not be being offered a sufficiently demanding curriculum. Through their identification as 'gifted' is is hoped that teachers will see their particular needs as having to be specially catered for. However, there are dangers about the labelling of children in this way and we discuss some of the potential difficulties later in the chapter.

Low-attaining children

There are low-attaining children who are not seen as having special needs. If your child is among these but is working conscientiously at his or her own pace in the class, and you and the teacher feel a steady rate of progress is being made, all is well. Though we have said that all children have gifts, they do not all have academic ones. We parents can give our children confidence in themselves, whatever their talents.

It may be that despite you and the teacher feeling school is okay for your child, they themselves feel frustrated at not doing better. If this happens, you do need to work out, with the teacher's help, how you can get your child to feel pleased about achievements so far, and confident about the next stage. National Curriculum assessment arrangements state that it is important that teachers should be constantly assessing pupils and that these and test results should contribute to a discussion of what happens next for each child. If your son or daughter is dispirited about their progress do not wait until the end of the term or year to ask for this kind of discussion. Some children, especially quiet ones, never share their concerns with the teacher, and the teacher will not know of their unhappiness unless you tell her.

Gifted children

It is our belief, as teachers and parents, that adults constantly and consistently underestimate children's capabilities. In our view it applies to all children. We do not mean that all children are 'gifted' in the official sense, but they all have gifts that exceed what adults perceive. It is certainly true of children with exceptional abilities and there is much research to support this.

The National Curriculum has been laid out in a series of Levels deliberately, so that once pupils have mastered all the concepts with one Level, they can progress to the next Level. However, there are problems with this. The first is that any class, whether it is a year group class or whether it spans more than a year, is likely to have within it children working at one of a range of three or more Levels. To plan work at all these Levels is difficult for a teacher of thirty-five or so children. If she also has to arrange an individual work programme in one or more subjects for the exceptional child, this is work for which she needs additional resources, including equipment, time and maybe even teaching skills. The second and perhaps more important problem is that teachers are often ill-equipped to spot exceptional ability, especially when the able child turns in scrappy work because he or she finds the topic dull and repetitive.

How do you spot, from the work the children are doing, outstanding performance or potential in specific academic areas, in problem-solving, in creativity and in physical skills? Despite giftedness being sometimes difficult to recognise and requiring special resourcing, classteachers are expected, under the National Curriculum, to provide opportunities for these children as for any other.

Teachers are wary and defensive of parents who go in to school to say their child is capable of harder work, or is not being stretched, or has exceptional ability. First they think we are being 'pushy' and putting undue pressure on our children, and secondly they may feel that they are in a better position to judge our children's performance when compared with other children of the same age. Both these views are valid. However, we are justified in asking the teacher to set more challenging work if we think it is appropriate, just to see how our children respond.

A cautionary note It is the case, as with the use of the 'special needs' label, that there is a growing use of the word 'gifted' which represents institutional attempts to categorise children. Along with the commonly assumed belief that there are about twenty per cent of children with special needs, there is a similar proportion who are 'gifted'. We see this as being unhelpful, and believe that a label such as gifted should be reserved for children with an exceptional talent, whether it be in mathematics, art, music or whatever. If your child is a high attainer, academically, then this will make some aspects of life easier and others harder. But from the child's viewpoint it is undesirable to elevate his or her capacity to something which may make the child appear different. It is, perhaps, a reluctance to admit that some children are clever that we are offered labels such as gifted. Well, some children are clever at sums and some are not but only a few are significantly different from what is seen as the 'normal' range. We also need to be cautious about the blanketing of children with a low attainment label, as this may lead them to live up to this lack of expectation. Far too often children are labelled according to their ability in English, particularly reading and writing, and other gifts or talents they have are subsequently under-valued.

CLASSROOM BEHAVIOUR AND CHILDREN'S NEEDS

There are occasions when all children demonstrate their unmet needs through their behaviour. Every child is sometimes aggressive, or has tempers, is underhand, or does things like flicking a pencil or nudging the child nearby. We can attempt to explain why children are 'naughty' or disruptive by looking at a range of possible reasons, including, for example, physical difficulties, food allergies, and emotional problems. It is, however, important for us parents to remember that the reasons for bad behaviour can be academic. There may not be a match between the children's ability and work set. Some children are naughty when the work is too difficult, some when it is too easy. If we bear this in mind, we can ensure this explanation is discussed if our own children become naughty at school. It is particularly important that teachers try to establish the reasons for repeated disruptive behaviour, because it not only disturbs the teaching plans of the teacher, but the learning of many other children.

SUMMARY

In primary school, the responsibilities of the teacher are to meet the needs of every child in her care. However, she does her work for them as a class, and there is little time to check that all is well, all the time, for every individual child.

We, their parents, are the most important people to ensure that they get what they need wherever they are, including at school. There are signs that we are honouring our responsibilities when our children:

- go willingly to school;

- look forward to (at least) some things at school;

- make academic progress in the opinion of the teacher;

- make academic progress in our opinion;

- make academic progress that they themselves acknowledge;

- get along with some teachers;

- get along with some children; and

- ask questions when they are uncertain or wish to learn more.

Throughout this chapter we have placed considerable stress on the responsibilities of parents and teachers, but we need also to appreciate that our children can contribute to meeting the needs of other children. They can and should, at the very least, allow their classmates to learn. They should also be given opportunities to extend the learning of others.

CONCLUSION

I n passing the Education Reform Act the Government has set in motion a series of changes, the effects of which will not be fully appreciated until the twenty-first century. The introduction of new ideas in education is a lengthy business, not least because it takes the school career of one set of children, that is eleven years, for the changes to have full effect. As parents we are keen to see the progress our children are making, but it is often the case that teaching cannot be measured in terms of short-term outcomes. Rather we have to wait for many years to fully appreciate what any particular teacher has offered our children. However, in the long-term interests of our children it is better that we take a rounded view of their development rather than focus on particular aspects of their current progress.

Ultimately, we believe that most parents are concerned that their children grow into responsible adults who have useful and happy lives. To help them achieve this we need to take a broad view of their schooling experiences, and this does not mean just letting them get on with it and being uninvolved. We would urge parents to appraise schools and teachers in the light of the total experience of their sons and daughters. The National Curriculum could help with this in that it offers a programme of activity and an agenda for action which is available to teacher and parent alike. We can enter into a dialogue which is not about what should be taught, but about what needs to be learned. This shift from the content of the curriculum to a discussion of the process of our child's learning might turn out to be the major benefit of a National Curriculum. Certainly, in this book we have consistently taken the view that the partnership between teachers, parents and children is what is of real and lasting importance in making the changes in education really work to good effect.

Schools no longer have a monopoly in terms of the knowledge available to our children. Rapid developments in technology have made childhood change in our lifetime. Home computers, compact disc players and, soon, interactive video players add to the explosion of information started through 'old' technologies like television! We all know stories from the 'olden' days, handed down from our parents and grandparents, about telephones, aeroplanes and cars. Now these stories are about hovercraft, jumbo jets, home cine films, and colour television. For our children to continue to have a real voice in the democratic process their understanding must move on in pace with technological innovation. Fortunately, however, there are human qualities which transcend this particular era. These qualities are the ones upon which we have built this book. They are to do with relationships, communication skills and the recognition of quality as against quantity.

In order to support and promote learning opportunities for our children, and their friends, we need to:

- understand the changes facing schools;

- know how to support our children's learning without imposing yesterday's criteria;

- be able to give praise where it is due;

- know how to ask for change and development without a breakdown of communication and goodwill;

- understand our children's strengths and weaknesses and help them to build on the former and overcome the latter;

- fight discrimination; and

- appreciate that the challenges of tomorrow need alternative views and responses from those of the past.

In taking an active interest in our children's education we have much to gain and nothing to lose. Whilst it is necessary to give over some of the responsibility of learning to teachers, it is essential that we do not abrogate our part in providing all-round educational opportunities.

We believe that the keynote of the immediate future can be partnership. We are coming through an age of individualism, to a point at which many of us see the need for cooperative activity. This cooperation is evident in our concerns about health care, protection of the environment and the promotion of international understanding and harmony. to redress these concerns and to produce an exemplary education system we need to be able to talk to and understand one another more, plan ahead and implement ideas in a considered way, and draw confidence from our friends and helpmates. Parents and teachers are guardians of the future and there is no job more onerous or rewarding than that. Together we can help new human beings to realise their considerable, but largely untapped, potential for personal growth in an increasingly interdependent world.

GLOSSARY TO THE NATIONAL CURRICULUM

Attainment Target (AT)	Part of a subject, it lists things children should learn, and is arranged in up to ten Levels.
Basic curriculum	The Foundation subjects together with Religious Education.
Continuous assessment	Judgements of children's progress made by the teacher on work done throughout the year using a variety of methods.
Core subjects	English, mathematics and science.
Education Reform Act 1988	The law setting out the National Curriculum for children in State schools in England and Wales. The Act also contains important changes concerning school management and governance.
Foundation subjects	The three Core subjects: English, mathematics and science, and seven others: technology, history, geography,

music, art and physical education; and a modern foreign language for children in secondary schools.

Key Stage

The four periods of schooling: up to age 7, 7–11, 11–14 and 14 to the end of compuslory education.

Level of Attainment

Attainment targets are made up of up to ten of these. Children should master one Level before going on to the next. Levels reached will vary from one Target to another.

National Curriculum

What is to be taught and learned in the Core and other Foundation subjects, and the assessment arrangements for these.

Profile Component

Attainment Targets are grouped in these for assessment and reporting.

Programmes of Study

What is to be taught in each subject in order that children may learn what is in the Attainment Targets.

Reporting ages

Also called Key or Assessment ages; they are 7, 11, 14, 16 when children are tested and their results given to parents.

Standard Assess- ment Task (SAT)

Tests given to children at the ends of Key Stages.

Statement of Attainment	Items for learning at each Level in each Attainment Target.
Statutory Order	Allows additions to and updating of the Education Reform Act.
Teacher assessment	Judgements of children's progress made by teachers.
Whole curriculum	Foundation subjects, religious education and other things taught.

INDEX